A Tour of Bones

A Tour of Bones

Facing Fear and Looking for Life

Denise Inge

BLOOMSBURY

LONDON • NEW DELHI • NEW YORK • SYDNEY

First published in Great Britain 2014

A Continuum book

Bloomsbury Publishing Plc
50 Bedford Square
London WC1B 3DP

www.bloomsbury.com

Bloomsbury is a trademark of Bloomsbury Publishing Plc

Bloomsbury Publishing, London, New Delhi, New York and Sydney

A CIP record for this book is available from the British Library

ISBN 9781472913074

10 9 8 7 6 5 4 3 2 1

Typeset by Fakenham Prepress Solutions, Fakenham, Norfolk NR21 8NN

Printed and bound in Great Britain by CPI Group (UK) Ltd, Croydon CR0 4YY

For Eleanor and Olivia,
daughters of my heart

Contents

1

The Charnel House

I live over dead men's bones. Dead women's, too, for all I know. Every day when I leave my house to escort my children to school, I walk over them. Beneath my hectic life they lie, dormant, deteriorating in increments, shifting perhaps imperceptibly when the ground around them shivers. In a perfect unity of name and action that I cannot begin to emulate, they do what they are, they remain. They make no noise about it. They insist on nothing, demand or require nothing of me except the admission, which I make seldom and reluctantly, that one day I shall join them in bare beauty, stripped even of flesh and sinews, disjointed, naked and alone.

* * *

How I came to be living in a house with a charnel house attached to it is a long story. My eighteenth-century Mennonite ancestors who ploughed out their Pennsylvania furrow in Plain Folk bonnets and beards, eschewing electricity when it came, disavowing the automobile, would no doubt be dismayed to see me returned from America to England, savouring traditions they found repugnant, finding in the old world a new and unexpected liberty. 'Way leads on to way', I think I'd tell them, calling on a poet from my childhood, Robert Frost. You fall in love with countries and with people; sometimes unexpectedly you fall in love with a life. Before you know it half that life is spent. 'Two roads diverged in a yellow wood', I'd answer, and I could not travel both.

You never know where a small decision will take you. You never know. I came to England as a tourist to find out what moors and hedgerows were. I came to cycle in Oxford and punt on the Cam, and to ride a double-decker bus. Loud and shy, taking up too much room on the sidewalks and unfamiliar with a pint of beer, I learned English things like cream tea and scones, and how to make custard, and that part of loving summer is to love the sharp thwack of a cricket ball on willow wood. I learned to pull the velvet sally on a bell rope. I made some friends and joined a religious community and eventually figured out how to light gas fires without them exploding and to drive on the other side of the road.

Then one January day, stranded in London by a freak snowstorm, I phoned a friend of a friend who had room in a house he shared that was not far away; he said I could weather out the storm, and that became my future. Not immediately of course, because he had given himself to God and I was going to teach in Casablanca and learn French. We parted bravely and declared our long-distance love in letters of the kind that won't exist any more now that people spell their luv by 'thnx 4 2day' and 'i m so in2 u'. Ours were paper letters which one opened crisply with a slice, and which crossed and double-crossed slowly in Moroccan mail, confusing us both so badly that we parted.

When the thin blue aerogram came to say he thought he should remain single I posted a blistering reply, the tone of which I regretted even as the finality of its soft thud sounded in the bottom of the box. I sat by that yellow postbox till the postman came but failed to secure the letter I could not prove was mine, whereupon I saw no recourse but to buy a tawny bottle of whisky from the pay packet I had been given that day and hand the entire remainder of my monthly salary, in cash in its long white envelope, to the beggar stationed on the cracked pavement outside the squeaking glass door of the seedy off-licence on *Boulevard des Almohades*. It made him weep with ecstasy from his torn bit of cardboard, and left me not only severely hung-over for days but also penniless for an entire month, during which I recomposed myself and decided to stop over in London to say a polite rather than confrontational goodbye before heading back to America for good. But nothing goes according to plan. He introduced me to his family. Instead of a polite farewell there was a sunny summer after which eventually I married him, and my original tourist trip that had already turned into several years became forever.

I have since acclimatized my way through decades until, suddenly, I find I have lived as long in England as I ever did in America, and am rooted in an English way of life. America, meanwhile, has gone on changing in my absence so that I am now almost as strange to it as I once was to England. Not entirely at home in either, not quite alien, I belong temporarily wherever I reside, which being married to an Anglican clergyman means possibly anywhere. Right now it means a large townhouse next to the cathedral and overlooking the river Severn in Worcester with a curious history including dereliction, crusty canons, ladies in crinolines, Sir Edward Elgar, Izaak Walton, medieval wayfarers, Benedictine monks and several hundred sheltering skeletons.

* * *

When my guests arrive, the wide front door swings open smoothly on its beautifully balanced hinges. They pass a velvet-trimmed curtain and step into a stone-flagged hall with high ceilings and in winter, if we are lucky, a roaring fire. They are welcome. Crossing this threshold, they have also stepped over dead men's bones. Even my bright-eyed puppy who, being a dog, ought to have a sixth sense about bones, pays them no heed. When I stop to think about this, which I have only recently begun to do, it seems strange to me that none of this, the door through which we have stepped, the floor on which we walk, the medieval stone foundations out of which the later brick elevations rise, would be here were it not for the bones below.

This townhouse was built exactly on the foundations of an earlier medieval dwelling that housed the charnel house priest whose job it was to pray for the souls of the departed. The term 'charnel house' comes from the Latin *carnalis*, meaning flesh. 'Ossuary' is another term, from the Latin *os* for bone. The Germans call it *Beinhaus*, or bone house, which is the most straightforward term I have come across, since a charnel house is exactly that. In past times, a charnel house was a simple solution to the practical problem of what to do with the unrelenting accretion of human remains. Many of the European charnel houses are medieval; some the result of physical changes to cities in the late eighteenth and early nineteenth centuries. Others are the result of plagues or wars. Few of them are still receiving new bones, as ours occasionally is.

The imprint of that medieval priest's house became the blueprint for this one, its previous presence the justification for construction. The whole reason our house exists, in this particular place, in this shape, is because there once lived a priest given the task of praying for the souls of those whose bones rested here beneath his own each night. He and the bones were brothers. Brothers in the monastic sense, because the charnel house and its priest were part of a Benedictine Abbey that included Worcester Cathedral, which is just next door, and the bones would have belonged to his fellow monks; but brothers too in a philosophical sense, because he lived with a constant sense of connection to those who had gone wherever souls go and left their bones behind. His house and its small chapel were a kind of left luggage room on a spiritual railway bearing always an expectation of return or reunion. At the resurrection of the dead these bones would live again with bodies more beautiful and more whole than any could imagine. And his would be among them.

Few of us live with such a perfect expectation. Many believe in an afterlife, some believe in nothing at all, but few have a well-developed notion of what life after the resurrection might mean, who we may find there, or what the terms of our relating to each other might be. The footprint of his house and mine is the same but I walk in it as in a pair of outsize shoes, aware always that our modern way of thinking has created slippage where medieval security might have been. Maybe I am wrong; maybe little about the unprovable afterlife has ever been secure, even in a medieval monastery, and that is precisely why he was given the job of praying.

Our cellar is all that remains of that medieval house. The least elegant part of the house, it is nevertheless the most intriguing for me with its two staircases, its small steps up and down, and its odd turns into many mysterious storerooms. At the front, stone mullioned windows shed rectangles of light on lime-washed walls and uneven floors; one step up leads you to the ping-pong playroom with overhead beams and a sloping floor. At the back, beyond a high threshold and a lockable door, lies the vaulted wine store with hooks for hanging hams, and shelves of higgledy-piggledy pots of mulberry jam, whisky marmalade and plum chutney. Along a corridor and up a short brick staircase you reach the laundry with its large stone sink so cold it turns your hands the chapped puce of a Victorian laundress's.

I love our quirky cellar, fell for it instantly. There is something so brave and purposeful about it. Over the centuries it has been changed but never given the kind of elegant facelift that the more modern public rooms of the house above have been given. It does not dissemble. There where ancient stone gives way haphazardly to seventeenth-century brick it tells its stories candidly – there where the sawed-off pipe of a disused tap remains, where a dog before ours chewed a door edge, where a handle broke and was replaced with a bit of old rope, where the key to a padlock was lost and a new one fitted and the brace and clasp of the old one left. Gouges in the wall tell where the old range stood, replaced by the unsightly but necessary reinforced steel girder that supports the present cast-iron Aga overhead. Only in the last room you come to does our honest and hardworking cellar conceal. There, under a rug that our young daughters have never lifted, lies the trap door.

* * *

From this belly of our house I began a kind of quest into fear so that I might overcome it and learn about living life unfrightened. It seemed brave at the time, and in a way it was if you imagine the kind of blind bravery with which soldiers have for thousands of years enlisted, innocent of battle terror. The scimitar, the bayonet, the trenches – these teach those who survive them more about courage and fear than they ever hoped to know. So it was for me. I started this book scared of the skeletons in my cellar. Before I had finished it I looked scarcely more than a skeleton myself, emaciated by cancer and chemotherapy. And I still do not know whether or not I am to be 'a survivor'. There is a tumour wrapped around my portal vein, my hypatic artery and my bile duct. It is inoperable; the surgery would kill me. It has been shrinking now for several months, and chemo has stopped. I can eat again, and carry things and swim and even laugh. I stand in the sunlight whenever the sun appears and let it bless me. Hundreds of people are praying for me.

I pray too and I hope. But nothing is certain. I try complementary treatments and a strict diet that I believe are helping my body to heal. I believe I will see my children to adulthood and beyond. I believe I will finish this book.

Shocking as it has been and is, what I am dealing with is not so different from what every single one of us faces. I am simply facing it in technicolor. With death it is not a question of 'if', only 'when'. And none of us knows the answer to that. We are all living with more unknowns than we like to admit. Independence, choice, autonomy, those qualities we value so highly that we pretend life is not worth living without, are largely illusory. Oh we have choices, certainly, but they are all made, and many of them can be unmade, according to and surrounding events over which we have no control. And what are we then, when we are no longer 'in charge'? We are free, I believe, if we can find it on the inside. Which is the only place from which freedom cannot be wrested, and the only kind of freedom that is abiding.

What seems so strange to me is that I wrote almost every word of this book before I was diagnosed with cancer. Did meditating on mortality somehow conjure the disease? I don't think so. But I do think in some ways it prepared me for it. Contemplating mortality is not about being prepared to die, it is about being prepared to live. And that is what I am doing now, more freely and more fully than I have since childhood. The cancer has not made life more precious – that would make it seem like something fragile to lock away in the cupboard. No, it has made it more delicious.

But this is not primarily a book about cancer and recovery. It's too early for that. This is about facing the fear of death. Looking the greatest fears full in the face can open up the cupboards of your life and throw the dust out. I began to discover this even before the cancer came. I discovered it on a tour of bones that started in my very own home. It is a strange tour, I admit, and one I never would have taken if it hadn't been for the fact of my slightly freaky cellar.

* * *

I have always half-liked being frightened. Navigating a posse of campers through snake-infested rivers of the New Jersey Pine Barrens I sang lustily though my heart raced at every paddle-stroke. I loved ghost stories told around the campfire, or high-level assault courses, or rappelling down rock faces. I have tombstoned into the icy waters of West Virginia lakes, and let the turbaned snake charmer in Marrakesh's Djemma El Fna bid me kiss the serpent he had wrapped around my neck. Largely weightless, these thrilling experiences of fear asked no unanswerable questions. They were not illusory, but they were pretend.

Serious danger is different. One time, when I was about nine, a dark lake's water, green and cold, closed over me and I fought for air; there was a bigger girl up towards the light with straggly hair whom I nearly drowned in my grip, struggling towards the surface. That incident my body remembers like a tattoo on the inside of my skin.

Other times, later, when I had grown up and started to travel, I also knew I was a whisker away from being swallowed – lost in the middle of the Sahara, the land rover broken down, and we started making calculations on the containers of water. Or in Morocco, when I yanked my arm free from the man who grabbed it to shove me into the back of a shiny black sedan with his three friends in a momentarily desolate boulevard in the industrial end of Casablanca one Saturday morning. '*Pas de problème*', they said, smiling, '*Mackai mushti*'; three men in smart suits, opening the door as if they were gentlemen.

I still remember the strange adrenalin strength of my arm, the single-mindedness that thought plainly, simply, this: get arm free, don't take the alley, stay where people can see you. In words of one syllable my mind made its plan: 'better dead this way', it said, setting my feet out into the traffic of the no longer empty boulevard where three lanes of cars now screeched to a halt and dozens of eyes were suddenly upon me, the strange pale blonde woman with wild eyes scanning jammed-up traffic for a bright red taxi.

I remember my skinny arm waving, my run the wrong way up through stopped traffic to where an incredulous driver bid me join his bleeding fare on the way to hospital. With so many witnesses my abductors had ducked back into their black car and dissolved, yet my hands, my legs would not stop shaking. Blood from the injured man's hand was pouring too generously on the taxi floor. A factory injury. Working overtime. So many ways to die here, I thought, wishing I knew something more useful than English, nursing perhaps, or even elementary first aid; wishing I had something, anything, to wrap around the grimy shred of rag that he pressed pitifully to his hand. I remember finding in my bag neat unpleated tissues that drank their fill in seconds and fell like crushed roses to the floor. The taxi driver's sweat, his courteousness in the blood and heat, the urgency of his wish to deliver me up unbloodied to a fashionable suburban street or a boutique boulevard, and the way I insisted, fruitlessly, that he take the injured man to hospital first. He would not.

'But he is bleeding', I pleaded.

'There are many accidents', he replied. 'Shall I take you to *Boulevard Mohammed Cinque*?' At the first inhabited street where there might be something other than closed factories I lied and said that I had reached my destination.

'*A l'hôpital vite, vite*', I urged, rummaging for notes in my wallet. The walking did me good, took some of the tremble from my limbs. I walked and walked through unknown streets knowing I would eventually come to something familiar, hoping the factory man I had last seen rocking in pain in the back seat, holding his hand fastidiously over the floor so as not to bloody the seat, was treated kindly.

That time I moved quickly in fear; I have also frozen in fear. I remember, for instance, the spot where three jeeps surrounded me at the border of Niger, men shouting, their mounted machine guns pointed at my breast, my back, my feet. I remember the bright light shone in my face and the quick decision to freeze lest any movement from me trigger a reaction from them. I remember closing my eyes in the blinding beam of light, then opening them slowly to face my fate, making myself look past the guns to their human faces. I remember being perfectly still and suddenly aware of the preciousness of my breathing, the value of my lungs.

There are other fears that take you silently. When you fear that the disease that nearly killed you may still be lurking in your bones, when you fear that you are not far from losing your grip on what is normally recognized as sanity by the myriad others that hammer the pavements beside you, courage alone will not alter the outcome. These are fears that never go away. Banished, but not executed, they skulk in the dark borders that are patrolled by will and instinct, liquid as shadows.

There is a final fear, quiet as cat's feet, which sits in the heart of everyone. We think we are toying with it when we tombstone from a cliff into the icy lake, but it has toyed with us. We think we have avoided it when we fill our days with ceaseless activity, but it is not conquered. It has infinite patience. It has inevitability on its side. This is the fear, heavy as a tomb, that I sense when I enter the charnel house.

* * *

No one likes to talk about death, almost no one knows how to. Those who do have mostly learned like you learn anything, by practice, because their jobs put them in situations where they meet people who are near the end of their lives. Yet spending hours at the bedside of dying persons does not necessarily give you any skill in death talk. Priests can make a terrible mess of funerals. Undertakers are past masters at avoiding the 'D' word with their impressive vocabulary of obfuscatory 'loved ones' and 'crossed overs' and 'departeds'. Doctors can be remarkably detached from mortal considerations.

I was talking about this one day with one of my oldest friends, Rachel, who is a consultant in palliative medicine. Her years of working with the dying have confirmed her suspicion that death has become a topic that no one wants to discuss. 'Despite taking time to consider a good car, a good house or a good school, we don't want to consider what would be a "good" death', she says. 'Death has become a medical condition rather than a natural end. It takes place more and more in hospitals and less in homes. Therefore people (including children) have less experience of dying and death; it becomes something to be feared behind closed doors – and what we don't see, we fear.'

Added to this increasing invisibility of death is the increasing success of treatments. As modern medical advances make more diseases and conditions manageable and curable, we come to believe that death is an appointment we can postpone. As Rachel put it, 'Death is seen as a failure both by professionals and, increasingly, by families.' This resonates with an article I read recently in *The Times*, by the American author Dr Pauline Chen: 'Patient death, for many doctors, represents a kind of failure, and so without really thinking, we look the other way.' The same thing happens in families, in marriages, in friendships.

We avoid talking about death largely because such conversations are painful, because death is brutal, because separation is unbearable, because we are heading out into a dark unknown. All of this is completely understandable. Perhaps we avoid it also because we fear we may find limits to our love. We don't know what to do when the forever we have promised ceases to be attached to the physical frame of the person we love. Where does that forever go? And if 'forever' means nothing more than 'in my lifetime', wouldn't it be better translated as 'for a while'?

Such a bounded view of human love is repugnant to many, and the great poets refute it. For them love is the stuff of life, a love that burns and turns, forever changing and forever new. Philosophers too have tried to answer our questions about the eternal nature of love. In Plato's *Dialogues* it is at the summit of love that the lover catches a vision of eternal beauty. This love, says Plato, draws us towards that which is most enduring. We humans are creatures attached to both worlds, the physical or 'sensible', as ancient philosophers termed it, and the eternal – if we possessed the eternal we would no longer be human; if we had no yearning for it we would be merely animal.

As the ancient philosopher Diotima shows in her dialogue with Socrates in the *Symposium*, love is one of the links between these worlds. She notes in particular the business of procreation: 'in procreation and bringing to birth the mortal creature is endowed with a touch of immortality, because procreation is the nearest thing to perpetuity and immortality that a mortal being can attain.' What is true at a physical level is even truer, she argues, at a spiritual level. The highest forms of love occur in the marriage of noble minds. This too is *eros*, though the concept may sound strange to modern ears. Whether physical or spiritual, love for Plato is linked with immortality.

We know that human love often fails, yet we see that for some people it endures. We yearn to be among that happy few. Our flesh may rot but we want our love at least to be immortal. Shakespeare's sonnets, Rodin's 'Kiss', the Taj Mahal all say so. In monuments of verse and stone our best artists have decreed that love is eternal. In our loving, the great human yearning towards eternity is voiced and sanctified. Yet we only come to know this when love is set in parameters of birth and death. Living love is enjoyed; it is only after death that love becomes immortal. And if love is immortal, is the beloved immortal also? These questions go right to the heart of how we understand ourselves. Much of the time, we pretend that death isn't a part of life. Yet, death is a crucial part of the human condition; when we avoid talking about death we avoid talking about life. This is what the bones in my cellar are telling me. Look at us, they say. Are we all that remains? Cancer or not, you will be like us one day. And what will be left of you then?

* * *

When someone's heart stops pumping blood around their body, the tissues and cells are deprived of oxygen and rapidly begin to die. But different cells die at different rates. Brain cells die within three to seven minutes, for example, while skin cells can be taken from a dead body for up to 24 hours after death and still grow normally in a laboratory culture. In the moderate climates of the Western hemisphere, it takes about twelve months for a human body to rot down to bone. It may take centuries for that bone to become dust.

The body has its own intrinsic method of breaking itself down. Micro organisms such as clostridia and coliform bacteria begin the decomposition process in the intestines before invading other parts of the body. The pancreas, packed with digestive enzymes, rapidly digests itself. Curiously, the organs where life begins, the uterus and the prostate glands, are more resistant to decomposition and last longer. But within a year all that is usually left is the skeleton and teeth with traces of tissue on them.

It takes half a century for the bones to become dry and brittle in a coffin. In neutral soil bones may last for hundreds of years, while acid soil dissolves bones more rapidly; and when there is free access to air a body decomposes twice as fast as when immersed in water and eight times faster than if buried in the earth. Humidity, temperature, clothing, time of year all play their part, but the most important variable is the body's accessibility to insects, particularly flies. A fully fleshed body left on the surface in the tropics can easily be reduced to clean bones in under two weeks.

Stone crypts sometimes provide just the right conditions for natural mummification, such as occurred in the catacombs of the Franciscan Brotherhood in Tolosa, Spain, or the Capuchin monastery in Brno, Moravia, or Klatovy in the Czech Republic. In these crypts dozens of monks and some lay people lie, with bricks beneath their heads and clothing still draped on their wizened skin. These sites share a natural constant temperature of about 59°F (15°C), and enough air movement to prevent vapour from the bodies building up in the crypts.

Another environment that favours mummification is freezing temperatures such as those found in upper altitudes in the Himalayas and Alps, as well as in the Arctic and Antarctic caps. The famous Otzi mummy (also known as 'Iceman') was found in the Tyrolean Alps in 1991, approximately 5,000 years after his death, in highly conserved conditions and still bearing the wounds of the weapon that killed him.

From the position of his fallen body and his wounds, it was possible to reconstruct a plausible crime scene 5,300 years after the murder. At the time of his death (aged 45) he was about 5 feet 5 inches tall (1.65m) and weighed roughly 110 pounds (50 kilos). Analysis of the contents of his intestines shows a diet of red deer and chamois meat, and processed einkorn grain, possibly bread, as well as fruits, roots and seeds: barley and flax and poppy seeds and the kernels of sloes and various wild berries. Pollen analysis discovered very well-preserved pollen of the hop-hornbeam, with cells intact, indicating that it was only a few hours old at the time of his death, which put his death in the spring. Since einkorn wheat is harvested in the late summer and sloes in the autumn, these must have been stored from the previous year.

He wore a cloak of woven grass and a coat, leggings, belt and loincloth of leather. His bearskin hat fastened beneath his chin with a leather strap and his shoes of bearskin and deer hide were water-proof and wide, with a curious kind of interior netting that created a space around the feet into which was stuffed soft grass for socks. He carried a copper axe, a flint knife and arrows, a longbow six feet (1.82 metres) long, medicinal fungus with antibacterial properties and tinder fungus, along with flints and pyrite for creating sparks.

X-rays and a CT scan taken in 2001 show that Otzi had an arrowhead lodged in his left shoulder when he died, and a matching small tear on his coat. The arrow's shaft had been removed before death. He had cuts and bruises on his hands and wrists and chest and had suffered a blow to his head. One of the cuts at the base of his thumb reached all the way to the bone and had happened so near his death as not to have had time to begin healing. We cannot be sure whether he died from blood loss in the shoulder or from a blow to the head – he could have fallen wounded, or been struck by an assailant.

Speculations about a struggle before death have been sparked by unpublished DNA analyses that claim to reveal traces of blood from four other people on his kit: one from his knife, two from the same arrowhead, and a fourth on his coat. The theories are that he may have killed two people with the same arrow, retrieving it on both occasions; and that the blood on his coat is that of a wounded comrade he carried on his back. His posture does not suggest an isolated death in which he expired from cold and blood loss; it looks as though, before death occurred and rigor mortis set in, he was turned face downward in an effort to remove the arrow shaft.

Reading his remains is like piecing together a puzzle, and which of us does not like figuring clues? But there is more to our interest than mere curiosity. We want to discover what he was like, which is another way of saying 'was he like us?' Implicit in the question of how he died is the related question of how he lived. Although we are unlikely ever to know whether he was chased because he was a rogue or a hero, it is not his innocence or culpability that make his story compelling. What matters is that he died cold, alone and hunted. We wonder what sort of life brought him to this frightening end, from what he was running, and to what refuge he was headed. In these questions we see ourselves, subject to the same hunger and cold, to fear and to pain.

Some of my newest neighbours will have been murdered ones. Not monks this time, but a collection of Anglo-Saxons who were found several years ago under the floor of the cathedral's chapter house during excavation for recent building works. Whenever builders unearth something of archaeological interest at sites as ancient as this, a full study of the discovery has to be made before the site can be covered over again. In this case the skeletons were exhumed in order to be examined. Quite by chance I saw these skeletons when we came to Worcester for the day during a half-term holiday not long after they had first been exhumed.

Having wandered round the cathedral that day, we had passed through the heavy oak doors at the side of the cathedral that lead into the cloister, a covered walk with carved stone arches and a black and white stone floor constructed round a square courtyard. On one side the arches were filled with stone to create a solid wall, on the other side strong beams of light fell through spanning arches that faced onto the courtyard's herb garden. Historically these arches, which are now filled with glass, would have been open and monks would have moved round the cloister to follow the sun as they studied or painted their illuminated manuscripts. On that October day we arrived to see the cloister home to tables of hungry tourists, the overflow of the cathedral café.

As you walk around the cloister square, doors lead off into various formerly monastic rooms – to the Great Hall for dining, or to a canon's house, or to the modern cathedral's café – and one door leads to the chapter house, the room in which governing monks (known as the Chapter) would have met to discuss monastery business. Round and tall with a high vaulted ceiling and clear lancet windows, the Worcester chapter house is a perfect specimen of a monastic council chamber. Stone seats wrap all around the perimeter wall in one continuous curving bench, save for where a large fireplace breaks the continuity for a burst of warmth. One central pillar holds the fanning arches in place.

At eye level all is stone; the clear glass windows which run along two-thirds of the chapter house walls are placed high up so that although the room is flooded with light no one can see in and no one can see out. There would have been no distractions from the business at hand. The acoustics here are pleasingly resonant. As the sound wraps around, the echo of a confident hum can be heard for four seconds. You can imagine a whisper of complaint from one novice to another becoming an unintended confession in the ears of an alert abbot on the other side. When empty it can be a place of great tranquillity. On Sundays after the 10.30 a.m. service it is full of running children and tea trolleys and a chatty queue for cakes.

On that autumn day however, when we happened upon it, it had been eerily quiet, though densely peopled with the living and the dead. Carefully exhumed bones had been laid out on tables over which busy people in white coats were peering, prodding the stark white bones with silver tools. Bold bands of sunlight ran diagonally from the clerestory windows over these bent backs and supine skeletons, bleaching the femurs and tibia, the light flashing off the small silver tools, airy particles hanging like gold dust in the shafts of refulgent light.

I remember standing in the half-open door, peering in, feeling fascinated and excluded less by an edict than by my own slight horror of seeing skeleton after skeleton laid out in such proximity. 'Shhh', I had said, by instinct, to my also curious, peering daughter; something reverent was happening. Among that ancient stone and calcium and modern steel, in the bright beams of light, able hands were moving; human hands on human bones hunting hints and clues, scraps of facts by which piecemeal fragments are stitched into a history. Here were people examining another person's bones – whitish-grey and ivory shaded to charcoal and some of them speckled a strange purplish hue – in search of that other person's past. To me it seemed that what these archaeologists were holding, touching, breathing in was as much their own future.

Quietly we had closed the chapter house door and left. Our footfalls on the black and white cloister floor had sounded loud as we had walked towards and through the dark stone tunnel that led out to a bright arch of light. Emerging to the cathedral precincts where golden-leaved trees guarded the deep green grass of College Green, we had seen children in navy blue blazers about to be let out of school for the day, little ones on bicycles, a white waddling duck. Everything had looked safe and happy.

'What a nice place to be a child in', I had thought, with not the faintest idea that within two years this city would be our home and this very spot a place we passed every day on our way to school. Without the faintest notion that those white bones laid out on tables carefully, skeleton after skeleton, were destined for my cellar. In the intervening years between that chance October visit and now, they have been in London to be studied further. I am told they will come to us neatly labelled, in boxes that will slot into our charnel house like luggage.

Not long after we moved into our house, I attended a lecture of the Worcester Cathedral Archaeological Society where Professor Tony Waldron was speaking about those Anglo-Saxon remains. I went to the lecture chiefly to be introduced to these future neighbours and found that half of the bones are those of children, eighty-one of them under the age of 15; of these children, 38 are foetuses, still-borns and infants.

So many sorrows. My mother's mind boggles at the strength that must have been needed to sustain such repeated losses. I feel that I want to make a soft place in the charnel house for these particular bones, I want to place them in white cotton and silk, tread softly as I head for the exit, be gentle with the latch. I want to tell their long-dead mothers they will be all right with me. As if that would mean anything. As if, even were they alive, it could assuage a single wave of parental grief. Perhaps their grief was different. Perhaps life was so hard that these parents expected to endure the loss of children as one loss among many: the general loss of health, the loss of sight, of hearing, of mobility, of teeth – an inexorable descent from vitality to decrepitude. Or perhaps grief is always the same regardless of culture or time, and frequency does not dilute its potency.

There are adult bones among them telling their own stories. Where children's lives were often short, adult life must have been excruciating. Dental hygiene was appalling. Many of the Anglo-Saxon jaws are pocked and pierced with holes eaten into and even through the bone by the poisonous juice of abscesses.

There is one woman whose badly bowed tibias show the signs of Paget's disease, a condition in which the natural regeneration of bone is greatly accelerated so that the old bone deteriorates before the new growing bone has had time to harden. Pagety bone is unable to withstand stress and the bones of persons with Paget's disease simply bend under normal human weight; then, as they harden, they harden to deformity. Not only were this woman's legs bowed, but the mechanics of her ankle joint had altered. If she walked at all she would have had a peculiar and painful gait.

Other injuries are recorded in the bones that are coming to us. Fractures on one of the neonate skeletons suggests it was abused, perhaps abandoned at birth. Several of the adult skulls have been split by blows to the head – warriors or villains, we will never know, but murdered all the same. One head, severed completely and laid on its chest in burial, may or may not have been executed. The unborn, the tiny, the unwanted, the lame, the murdered, the criminal or maybe the merely calumniated – they are all coming to stay with me. Despite multiple tests and speculations, no one knows why some of their skulls have turned lavender.

* * *

I knew before we moved here about the charnel house. That detail came on page eleven of the dossier of documents which we were given when my husband was appointed to his post. The house goes with that appointment; when you accept the post, you tacitly accept the house. It is not negotiable. So there is no point in letting yourself be scared of a thing like a charnel house, which in any case is nothing more than an irregular rectangular box marked on a floor plan amid the pages detailing moving procedures and architect's drawings of the front and rear elevations of the house.

Since an episcopal appointment is confidential until publicly announced, we could not visit the house until shortly before we were to live in it, but these papers helped us begin to imagine *how* we might live in it – who would sleep in which bedroom, where the larger pieces of furniture would fit – and gave us a framework for discussion as we planned our future together in the closeted intimacy of a secret.

Much of what we imagined was wrong once we got here – dossiers tell you nothing of how light falls in a room, or which room is cold as a witch's grin, of the impracticalities of corners and the charm of niches – but it helped nevertheless. We were reliably informed, for instance, that the hall was large enough for the piano, that the kitchen/family room was easy and open plan, that the drawing room was located upstairs, that we would have one guest room; and we also knew that there was a charnel house in the cellar. These were simple facts, and there was so much effort required once we moved just to unpack and settle in that we didn't even consider investigating the charnel house until we had lived here for several months.

Then, late one evening when the children were sound asleep, the inquisitive cousins who were staying with us asked, after dinner, if we might all go see the charnel house. Why not, we thought; we'd been meaning to for ages. I wasn't scared. Besides, we also had a friend staying who is a Benedictine monk. It seemed only right that he should be among the first to visit the charnel house full of his Benedictine brothers. The torches in our house, usually having been either left on by children till the batteries run dead or abandoned in the garden, are notoriously unreliable. So armed with candles and matches we descended to the cellar, filed into the final room, rolled the rug back and slid a long-handled flat-nosed screwdriver under the edge of the trap door.

There is no wooden door with wheezing hinges, no ancient lock. There are no bunks like shelves; I had expected death, but thought there would be dignity. There was none of that. On three sides are earth and stone. On the fourth, a low opening cut beyond which there is only darkness. This solo journey is begun not with a bold stride but with a shrinking tuck: you must duck your head considerably to pass through the narrow block opening. A candle passed ahead of you into the space reveals a further short drop over the threshold, and what looks like an uneven earthen floor.

It is not far. You can lower yourself with ease. Except that the floor is slightly sloping and there is nothing to hold onto and you do not want to fall, you really do not want to fall and find yourself tangled in a mass of bones, knee to a bleak shoulder bone, cheek to a stranger's skull. For the candle shows me too, as I duck my head and pass through, extending its small light out in front of me, that contrary to my expectation there are no bunks. There are no shelves. There are no neat bones. Instead, there is nothing here but the chaos of death: bones heaped on bones in disarray, indignity upon indignity, jaw upon pelvis, femur upon cranium, as if they had fallen into a freeze while wrestling at the moment the door was opened.

They lie in sloping piles that seem to reach almost to the arched stone ceiling that I can see as I raise the candle up. It is not far above my head. I see, in the banks of bones, smooth domes of skulls, grey and silver in the candlelight except where eyeless sockets dart their pitch-black stares. Even upside down, or with someone else's rib protruding through them, these sockets glare, dark and unblinking.

So far beyond care, so far beyond fear, they are strangely empowered. The things that remain. And there are so very many more of them than there are of me, or even of the friends and family whom I can hear chatting in the light of the small opening behind me.

I stretch my candle arm as far as it can reach, straining to see how deep the charnel house is, but I cannot see to its end, and I dare not step any further for bones and skulls have slid from their piles and there is no clear path. I do not want to step on the bones, but neither do I want to kick a clear passage through them. On every side are tumbled bones and crumbled stone. There is no decent air in there, but hundreds of years of dust.

'Just a bunch of bones,' I say to myself in the darkness, 'just a bit of dust.' But instinctively I have put my candle-free hand to my mouth so as not to breathe it in. I am afraid of the taste. I fear it will import with it some inexplicable mote of death to my lungs. I am disturbed by the chaos I see, saddened by the lack of dignity. I find myself torn: on the one hand I want to flee, on the other I feel an urge to stay and try to sort them out, arrange them at least in tidy piles – the skulls in one place, the pelvises in another. Pulling the spluttering candle towards my chest I duck back-first through the narrow opening and raise myself on trembling elbows out of the trap door pit. Everyone is laughing at a joke I could not hear from below. I blink.

* * *

This is really when the journey began. It did not start when the airplane landed in Prague, when, jaded and hungry from travel, I was joined by Zuzana, a multilingual Slovak friend who had agreed to be my interpreter and travelling companion; nor even in the weeks preceding when, buoyant as sea-voyagers hoping for adventure, we had laid out our maps, surfing the internet for relevant sites, chortling at translations like the advert from a hostel that invited us to 'fish our own trouts' which would be served to us by the host's 'roasted wife'. Or the hotel in Poland that proclaimed: 'We eat piglets. We drink beer. Only pleasant memories survive.'

Laughing, we had fled towards self-catering sites. One showed a ramshackle cottage jam-packed with artefacts and folk art, with a charming little garden rigged up with homemade canopies and recycled arches. If you were looking for local flavour you couldn't get better than this. We booked immediately, beginning an email correspondence with its owner Barbara, who made us feel as if we had been mistaken for angels with her idiosyncratic greeting, 'Halo girls'.

There are so many places we might have visited. The Paris catacombs where six million bodies line 300 kilometres of tunnels, the Capuchin crypt beneath the church of Santa Maria della Concezione in Rome where the bones of 4,000 monks decorate the walls. Even more macabre, the Capuchin catacomb of Palermo, famous for its mummified remains dressed and waiting for the resurrection. These charnel houses are well known, but in fact there are thousands more – they occur all over the world. There are Christian, Jewish, Shinto, Buddhist and Zoroastrian charnel houses; some contain bones, some cremated remains. Recently in Brazil a charnel skyscraper has been built to house urns of ashes.

In fact, when I started investigating, I found so many charnel houses in so many places that I knew right from the start I would have to be clear about the purpose and limits of my journey. Goth tourism was not my aim. Befriending my own charnel house was, so we decided to look for charnel houses near to mine both geographically and culturally. This meant Europe. Even so there were far too many to attempt a comprehensive study. We hunted for little-known sites – the smaller and more remote the better.

At Czermna, a little hamlet on the Czech/Polish border, we came across a small bone chapel. Then we found Hallstatt, a UNESCO World Heritage Site on Hallstattersee in the Austrian Lake District, where the charnel house skulls are decorated and named. Then, completely off the tourist trail, a simple charnel house in Naters, a village near the town of Brig at the foot of the Simplon Pass, one of the most beautiful passes in the Alps, constructed by Napoleon for his troops. We broke the small and remote rule, however, for one charnel house that curiosity compelled us not to miss – the frankly freaky ossuary at Sedlec in the Czech Republic with its famous bone chandelier.

An itinerary was forming, but even this itinerary, concrete as it became, was not the start of the journey. It had started when I lowered myself into the pit, when I held my candle out into a darkness it could not completely dispel, when I did not kick the bones.

Previous occupants of the house had had the charnel house closed off; it was opened up before we moved in anticipation of the addition of new bones. This opened door in my house, between the humdrum everyday and heaped mortality, never stopped asking questions. I became curious about the way our disposal of bones has changed through time, and how this might reflect our changing attitudes to life, death and the hereafter – in fact, to our whole understanding of who we are as humans.

We are free at funerals to choose our own music, write our own liturgies, dispense with a grave altogether and be scattered. Or not to have a funeral at all. We are free, and somehow a little bit lost at the same time. Our aspiration for the enduring and even the infinite has not left us. The desire to remember and be remembered, far from abating, continues to be a basic part of being human. Human too is the belief in some hereafter which, despite all that we know about molecules, about decomposition and about the transitions of matter, remains in our imagination stubborn as an accidental ink-stain.

All of these things and more have come to me gradually, on swelling and shrinking tides of thought swept in and out of my mind during the journey from that first step into our charnel house to the farthest corners of Silesia and back again. If, since living in this house, I have thought more frequently about the brevity of life and the longevity of bones, I have also thought more about fear, about how all fears lead back to the fear of death – and how, if you are going to live an unfrightened life, you need to face that head on. I don't know exactly how you do this, but I suspect integrity and an unflinching mettle are required.

I have been on many travels, and I shall go on a few more, but the biggest journey for me right now, the one that challenges me most, is the interior one, a journey that goes deeper rather than longer. It starts by going physically deeper, going underground beneath my own house. I like that: when the physical and the spiritual meet, copy each other, speak in parallel. That is something I trust.

Have you ever participated in one of those group-building trust exercises in which you are invited to fall backwards into the arms of another person who, you are told, is waiting to catch you? I love those. And if done from a height, into the arms of several people, I like that even better for I have long loved the feeling of falling. Once, as a young child, I fell from a great height and the memory has never left me. Glorious falling, lightly flying, weightless, free, abandoned. (I blacked out before I landed and miraculously suffered no injury, so have no negative memories associated with this event, although I do remember vividly the thrilling ambulance ride to the hospital and the doctor there asking me to perform the ridiculously difficult task of peeing into a very small jar.)

That early experience of falling, like another of nearly drowning, had skewed my sense of risk and danger. You do not die, it told me: you pass through danger, thrilled and exhilarated. Of course I know that this is not true, or at least not ultimately so. But I had never fully shaken those early impressions that disconnected me from mortality. Cancer has dismantled that. The possibility of death is carried in my body, just as beneath my ordinary front door lie those skeletons. That is why I am so interested in them.

There is something bare about them that feels like truth to me. They are unadorned, unashamed, and uncompromising. I feel myself grow tall in these three words – and then I glimpse the Mennonite in me which prides itself in just such negatives, and feels rich when casting off the inessential. I see that what I crave is to chase the plain and simple things.

When the famous nineteenth-century American philosopher Henry David Thoreau went to live in his little cabin at Walden Pond, he wrote that he went to the woods because he 'wished to live deliberately'. He wanted to face the essential facts of life and, as he put it, 'see if I could not learn what it had to teach, and not, when I came to die, discover that I had not lived'. He did not want to live a superficial life, but to 'live deep and suck out all the marrow of life, to live so sturdily and Spartan-like as to put to rout all that was not life'.

This wish to live deliberately is a fierce wish. It took Thoreau into solitude and the study of nature, into contemplation and civil disobedience. It required him to search out the corners where life lived. Writing my way into this book I have realized that what often scares us about the brevity of life is the fear that we have not yet found those corners, or that we may not have truly lived, and may never live, before our time is run out. We fear we may miss our one brief moment. Thanks to our advancing skill at body repair, we live longer and longer. Yet we know, somewhere beneath the celebrations, that life is more than not dying.

This book of bones, despite its frequent skulls, is really a book about that life which is more than not dying. My paring-down stance does not consist, as did Thoreau's, in inhabiting a one-room cabin, on my own, in the middle of nature, tempting as that sometimes sounds. Instead, it consists in staying with the uncomfortable sight of bare bones until I fear neither them nor the message of mortality that they utter. It consists in looking at myself without the flesh on.

2

Czermna

The first leg of my journey will take me all the way to Czermna, a hamlet on the edge of a remote spa town in a distant corner of Europe that was once called Silesia – a region fought over by successive armies and attached to acquisitive empires. Hungry and tired, there I will meet with kindness and brutality; I will meet strangeness and forgiveness and not know how they are related. I will stay in one of the most curious houses I have ever seen. I will arrive there looking for answers, and I will come away haunted by a question.

It was a long way to Czermna. Even when you shrink the overland distance through France, Belgium, Germany and into the Czech Republic by flying the first 793 miles from London to Prague, still you have quite a way to go. It was not just the mileage but the distance, by which I mean the span of cultures, the alienation of strange words, the inscrutability of foreign food, the unfamiliarity of coins. Even the maps upon which we relied to guide us were a minefield of probable errors. I was stymied every time I tried to name a place – 'Czermna' was a hesitation on my lips. 'Kudowa Zdroj' with its w's that were v's and its j's that were y's. Well, what did I expect? I had intended strangeness.

In the silent months between conceiving the idea and embarking on the tour, I had stopped writing. I had stopped researching. I had tried (unsuccessfully) to stop thinking about the trip because I wanted everything to be fresh, to arrive to the unexpected and experience everything as new. We had chosen four charnel houses in four different countries, none of them familiar. I wanted to keep it that way, to be completely open as only a stranger can be to what the travelling and the destinations would say to me, to feel what those lines from a poem by the seventeenth-century poet Thomas Traherne are saying about seeing things for the first time:

> A Stranger here
> Strange Things doth meet, Strange Glories see;
> Strange Treasures lodg'd in this fair World appear,
> Strange all and New to me.

He is writing not about a traveller but about an infant, describing the newborn as first of all a stranger in the world. Maybe one of the things we humans love about travelling, I thought, is that it brings us these moments of innocence. Stunned by the new, our senses are keen, our minds are awake. In the wash of the unfamiliar we swim like newborn seals, graceless till we hit the water, eyes intent, surviving, imbibing, agog. Our new infancy is even more pronounced if we do not speak the language. Just like infants, we are deaf to all instruction, infringe regulations and live by example. Proud notions of independence dissolve.

Like infants too, travellers are often sleep-deprived, hungry and lost. They are easily deceived. The adult traveller submits to these indignities in the belief that the benefit of the new outweighs the trouble it takes to get to the place of newness, but when we plan our journeys we rarely consider the personal discomfort of adventure. Prague station, when we found it, seemed to speak directly into such discontinuities of place and time. Outside, broken pavements, graffiti, a stubborn front door – dreary remnants of failed socialism. Then, inside, shiny escalators swept us past electronic screens designating times and platforms, past a gleaming Burger King. Everything was in the process of construction; we dodged cones and builders carrying long metal tubes (who, if they had turned right or left, would have annihilated seven pedestrians in one fell swoop) before finding at last the gleaming row of ticket windows.

As if the transformation we had just witnessed from fractured history to chrome modernity were nothing but a film set, we emerged, blinking, to scruffy platforms where passengers in jaded jeans and faded anoraks waited, nonplussed by the shriek of the approaching train. My hands dropped the bags and flew to my ears in pain. I could not believe any rail company could be allowed to let their brakes get into such a parlous state; as the train drew to a stop the wail intensified, came underneath my fingernails and quivered up my nose. Then one woman in a smart business suit carrying what felt like the whole of modern capitalism on her shoulders strode along the platform, grabbed the side handle of a waiting train and hiked herself up, closing the ungainly gap between platform and footplate with the swing of a coltish leg and one black court shoe. Consulting our tickets again, we boarded behind her, hoping we had found the correct train that would take us away from the city east to Nachod near the Polish border; feeling anyway that, even if we were wrong, we would rather be going in her direction.

In the hours that followed, long-armed and easy, sun-drenched and dreamy, I nestled my head on the bristly headrest and thought, clickety-clack. About the human aversion to strangeness, clickety-clack, how we crave the known and familiar as deeply as we claim to love the shiny and new, clickety-click. How our favourite pairs of shoes for walking are the oldest, how we hoard and sentimentalize, scrapbook and memorize. How we are not only creatures of habit but also of history, without which we do not know ourselves. I wondered what it is like to live in a country where so much of that is changing so fast.

Now, as I sit at my desk and write, I begin to appreciate the necessity of strangeness, the importance of being taken beyond the boundaries of the familiar in order for new thoughts to appear. Then, looking out at the fast-passing countryside, all I did was drink it in, my mind searching always in the new for something familiar, something understood on which to hang the new impression, so that when we passed flat fields where workers harvested red rows of radiccio and bright lines of cos, I registered, familiar to me, the East Anglian Fens.

I looked out of the train at the passing failed socialist cityscapes and agrarian landscapes and did not know that out of these glimpses of culture and agriculture my mind was busily plaiting the visually familiar and the unfamiliar into a kind of mental refuge for my psyche. I didn't ask my brain to do this, didn't even know that's what it was doing. But it was putting up defences against the strange as fast as I was providing it with unexpected images. 'The power of the new, the shocking and the astonishing', writes Stephen Cherry in his recent book *Barefoot Disciple*, 'is that it somehow gets past our defences and starts to trouble us.' I know now, as I reflect on my journey, what he means.

I had not yet come to anything like the border of the new, though I had passed stations of the inexplicable. Like the stop after Lysá nad Labem where the train screeched to its ear-piercing stop in a ghost town of rusty roofs and spent lampposts. There, with dozens of abandoned freight cars littering the sidings, inertia settled upon the train in an eerie silence, as if we were waiting for the arrival of some determining force.

Suddenly and with wind-whipping speed, a train thundered past on the nearest line to ours, rattling like a tin of giant dominoes. We waited. A random passenger, glued into headphones, opened a door, descended directly to the tracks. 'Wait!' I wanted to call, remembering the train that had just passed us, 'Somebody stop him!' No one looked up from his luncheon roll as the man crossed five working lines and placidly disappeared over a ridge towards nothing. We opened the window to listen to the silence, and heard in this eerie hiatus birdsong sweet in the late spring air. Then, for no apparent reason, with a shudder and a thud our train wheezed to a start and trundled on. Nothing except the birds had made sense to me.

The further east we went, the odder things became until, arriving at Nachod on the Polish border, the supply of familiar so diminished that the neat plaiting of familiar and unfamiliar started to unravel. We had been travelling since 4.00 a.m. We'd had no time to stop for breakfast in the Prague station rush; at nonsensical Lysá nad Labem, we'd had no rolls to unpack while the savoury scents that pinged from the popped tins of our neighbours' paté had snaked across the aisles to torture us. It had been nearly twenty hours since our last meal. Heady with hunger, we spied with delight just outside the station a little wooden cabin called Bramborka, 'The Little Potato', selling all manner of potatoes – fried, chopped, made into pancakes, even potato sandwiches – and a choice of two hot drinks: punch and … 'Grog!' I exclaimed, laughing at the absurdity of this drink I had always imagined was reserved for pirates in storybooks. The person at the window of the cabin was not, however, a fellow pirate but a harried middle-aged woman in a sweatshirt and fat-splattered apron, a fish slice in her hand, waking me out of my dream with a question I could not understand but which seemed to require a swift reply.

Though I could read nothing, photographs of my culinary options were helpfully pasted to the walls of the Bramborka. Encased in damp plastic, they showed pictures of what I took to be mainly meaty things in bread rolls, various deep-fried chicken parts (though they could as easily be rabbit), and flat roundish shiny things that could be pizzas or pancakes, or might in fact be flying saucers. Although there was no queue behind me and little sign of one building in the near future, I was clearly taking too long to decide; the apron lady uttered crosser-sounding words than the first. I pointed at one of the flying saucer pancake pizzas and stuck my head into the window to watch. Would it come from the oven? A fat fryer? From a freezer? But the cabin was ill-lit and I could see little.

As I pulled my head back out I noticed four dark-haired gypsies around us and Zuzana urging my suitcase closer to the protection of my careless calves, but no threat was real to me. Nothing was quite real to me, or rather, one real thing did not relate to another. The sequential links by which we recognize our place in the familiar world were damaged here and I was increasingly left with a series of lucid but somewhat isolated impressions.

The grog arrived tawny and clear, steaming in its cheap plastic cup. Gingerly I drew it towards my face, my fingers pressing dimples into its flimsy sides. I sipped. Liquid heat torched my nose and eyes and throat all at once. I passed the cup towards Zuzana, who had been called back to the window for our order. Shiny and hot, my *bramborak* slid across the counter with greasy ease on a torn sheet of non-absorbent paper. Eyeing it suspiciously, I lifted it slowly in my fingers and bit. A little rubbery, I reflected, but not so bad really with a day's hunger behind you.

Even with some food inside us, Nachod continued to feel like an absurd theatre. We knew we had to catch a bus across the border to

Poland but the bus timetable appeared to run backwards, so that the bus which left Nachod at 16.45 arrived at Kudowa Zdroj at 16.25. I handed it to Zuzana in despair. The tall gypsy woman, ruby earrings glinting against her deep black hair, glared at us aggressively from the Bramborka bar. Her man downed his large bottle of beer and peered with benighted interest at the contents of his fellow's small pull-along wagon: one torn traffic cone, two packets of soap powder and a disembowelled white portable television. The value of these things was completely lost on me, as was the continuing attraction of the grog, although two loud lads arrived by farting car and queued for it with a relish amounting almost to glee.

Scanning eagerly for a sign, a word, anything familiar, my eyes lit upon a poster pasted among many on the wall of a nearby shop advertising classes where you could learn 'Magic English'. Foxed by the impossible bus timetable which suggested to us that we had already missed the last backwards bus of the day, I began to wish for anything magic or anything English that would help us get out of there and to a comfortable shelter for the night. Slippery *bramboraks* swallowed, we abandoned the remaining grog and approached a kind-looking woman with a toddler standing near the taxi rank. 'Yes, this is the taxi rank,' she said, 'but the taxis don't go from here.'

* * *

Nestled in the wooded foothills of the Stolowe Mountains, enriched by salt mines and served by thermal springs, Kudowa Zdroj is one of the oldest spa resorts in Europe. In 1580 mineral waters were noted in the region at Czermna in the Chronicles of Louis of Nachod. Decades later a seventeenth-century Lutheran monk wrote about the tasty mineral waters at Kudowa, their health-giving properties and their usefulness in wine-making. Such a treasure couldn't remain unclaimed, and the first official owner of the springs was Albrecht von Wallenstein, commander from the Thirty Years' War, the war that denuded the region of its trees, plundered its wealth and decimated its population. The public consumption of spa water gradually began.

As early as 1630 small shelters are known to have been constructed from wood to facilitate healing baths, and the first attempt at a scientific description of the baths was made in 1694. But it was not until nearly two hundred years later, after the first scientists and doctors had made a chemical analysis of the waters which suggested that they had healing properties for the cardiovascular and circulatory systems, that Kudowa became a popular destination for the nineteenth-century élite. Under their entrepreneurial eye, what had been a small healing fountain with little wooden cabins near a remote castle grew to a fully fledged thermal park with avenues of palms, box-edged beds opulently spilling flowers, and an arboretum of species trees.

In 1847 the spa was visited by three hundred patients. By 1900 the number was 4,150 and, with a railway, in 1906 the numbers doubled. Among Kudowa's most illustrious visitors were the courtier, diplomat, adviser to the Ottoman Empire and Commander of the Prussian Army, Helmut von Moltke and his family, and the wartime English Prime Minister Winston Churchill.

Kudowa is a place that has changed its name many times. From Lipolitov under the Hussites to Chudoba in the mid-sixteenth century, then Kudoba in the nineteenth century, it became Bad Kudowa during the period when it was part of Germany in the province of Lower Silesia, then Kudow Zdroj after 1945 when many German inhabitants were forced to leave and Polish settlers filled their places.

Despite the ravages of war, much of its nineteenth-century grandeur remains. Palm trees line the wide gravel paths that lead past indoor and outdoor concert halls, past the handsome rotunda that now houses the pump house. Beneath American pines, Japanese ginkgo and towering copper beeches, azaleas and rhodo-dendrons flash their bold bright blooms. Benches abound, paths meander up the side of the hill, the park growing wilder and steeper till it merges with woodland paths that lead eventually beyond the park to a high-level ropes course heavy with happy youths, and beyond that to the small village of Czermna. Despite all of this, Kudowa Zdroj is a quiet place. Its healing waters and tranquil hills have not yet hit the modern international tourist trail.

It seems they have not even hit the Czech tourist trail, for the taxi driver we eventually found, decrepit as his car, hunched wheezing over the wheel, seemed entirely lost once over the border. What was worse, between gasps, he recounted his recent release from hospital, the infuriating refusal of anything to work properly – the brake pads, his heart, the gearbox, his lungs. With each gasp and clutching at his chest, we feared both he and the taxi were on the brink of complete demise. 'Perhaps we should just stop here and get out', suggested Zuzana at the precarious bend of an unknown road. I glanced at the darkening sky and shook my head.

The taxi rattled ominously at the change of gears and groaned up the hills until either the driver or the car grew tired of trying. Dropping us unceremoniously by the side of an empty road somewhere outside Kudowa Zdroj, he declared us to be 'in Czermna'. This he said in English, pointing fiercely to the ground at our feet and repeating it twice in case we were in any doubt. Pocketing our *koruna* with obvious satisfaction, he lurched back into the car, banged the rusty door and clattered off, leaving us with a cloud of black exhaust and a sincere wish to be somewhere else, somewhere kind and warm and waterproof.

There were puddles in the gravelly grit at the roadside and clouds overhead. Evening was upon us. With no idea in which direction to go and a plucky hope that Barbara would still be waiting for us when we got there, Zuzana hoisted her backpack onto her shoulder blades, I yanked my pull-along into line and we trudged on. Keeping to the road climbing gently away from Kudowa Zdroj towards the hills, in the stillness of the evening countryside my noisy tag-along rumbled on the tarmac like a thunderous armadillo. We fed on hope and on humour, laughing at the folly of our city selves trundling along the road to nowhere, in approaching darkness, in a foreign land, with ridiculous baggage.

Eighteen colourful gnomes flashed their stone smiles at us from the garden of a concrete bungalow. After the gnome house a settlement, then street names appeared, and persons we could ask. Suddenly, from a pub across the road, a gang of shirtless young men vomited, brawling, into the street. One knelt on the chest of another at the side of the road, held his close-shaved head in line with any oncoming car and pummelled it. Bright blood spurted from his nose, scarlet ribbon on the gritty tarmac, and we stood transfixed by the force of that violence and the terrible potential of a car arriving suddenly over a hill in the dusk. Two neighbour ladies, clutching their cardigans, leaned over a gate absorbing the scene with curiosity and no alarm, adding it to their week's quota of quotidian gossip.

Shaken, we fled into a muddy side street. It was Chrobrego Street, where we hoped to find Barbara. Instead, she found us, sliding inexorably, arms flailing, through ever-deepening mud towards a neighbour's wire mesh fence. 'Halo girls!' she called, her smile in the dusky twilight as bright as the midday sun.

* * *

I was not prepared for Barbara, though Barbara had prepared a space for me. Short and round and cheerful, with grey-peppered hair yanked back and gathered into a small practical knot, the sleeves of her patterned jumper were too long, as if it belonged to her husband or her brother. She and Richard had been there for hours stoking the antediluvian coal-fired boiler; she had got out her best china for our tea. Countless times I have extended hospitality to visitors; now there I was, receiving. Receiving puts everything on someone else's terms. And the terms of Barbara's house were not terms with which I was familiar. There was not chaos in Barbara's house but a different kind of order. In a journey of increasing strangeness, stepping into Barbara's house took me past eccentric to the very edge of the absurd.

There were five let rooms in the house. Ours was number 16. Zuzana turned the key and we ducked to enter, finding ourselves in a low-hung room full as a second-hand furniture warehouse with a king-sized bed between marble-topped nightstands. Beside formica cupboards squeezed an ancient wireless and a beautiful antique child's sleigh on which perched a charmingly threadbare teddy.

'Would you like some tea or coffee?' Barbara called up the steep linoleum-lined stairs. Every surface in the house, I had noticed, horizontal or vertical, was covered with objects, paintings, carvings, hangings. Portraits abounded – particularly a primitive collection, painted on thin cut-outs of wood, with long Modigliani necks and faces.

My eyes ranged over everything in our room, fascinated by the wildly eclectic collection of pictures that bedecked the walls. Gulping images, I tried without success to make any kind of sense of their selection and arrangement – the ghastly and the exquisite given equal pride of place, the only apparent organizing factor for their position being the availability of space. Beautifully painted old ceramic tiles of peasant girls holding an arch of flowers hung next to faded Renoir prints, Japanese ladies painted in reverse on glass and socialist-realist peasant Holy Families. Over the double bed an erotic print showed a woman manacled to a rock, head thrown back in torturous ecstasy, fingers to her nipple, pleasuring herself. Next to her, lithographs of churches averted their eyes, and a nineteenth-century woodcutter ignored her and got on with his work.

My eyes drank on – a bleak hunter in winter, *La Bohémienne*, then Leda and the Swan coupling; two nineteenth-century Dutch women in black conversed at a table; Holy Mary held her child facing out to the world; another woman paused at an open gate waiting – for escape, for her lover, possibly for a letter. My brain called 'Enough!' but my eyes wanted to miss nothing of this jabber of human life, its agonies and ecstasies, its myths and lore, its transgressions and indefatigable hope.

The practical function of the room was no less bizarre. There were three kinds of curtains at the one window. None of them closed, though one at the top gave a credible imitation of Bo Peep's flounce. As it turned out, our giant bed was in fact two singles pushed together and rigged out in faux-four-poster style by fixing a narrow frame of gas pipes to the ceiling and draping bits of greying net curtain over them, fastened with small neon-bright plastic hairclips. The bed itself was made up in exquisite antique white embroidered bedclothes trimmed in handmade lace. What was inside the lumpy duvet cover we decided not to investigate. It might have been an ancient duvet; it may have been a collection of odd pillows or old teddy bears.

For the last 20-odd hours I had been rattled by planes and cars and trains, dumbed by foreign languages, famished, fed slippery potatoes and grog, glared at by a ruby-eared Romany, dumped at a violent roadside, taken further and further from anything familiar and ended up here in the queerest house an absurd fairytale could invent. Anything could happen next. From any one of the squeezed-in wardrobes, trolls or bandits or giant German-speaking gummy bears could emerge. I would not have been surprised to discover that the second staircase led into a cavern or the nest of a phoenix.

The loo, it seemed, was down a long corridor constructed in the eaves of the house. You ducked, felt your way past head-bashing beams. An acid yellow cistern in dispute with its bowl, topped with a hot-pink plastic seat. The sliding door and cramped quarters made me feel I was still on the train and I half-expected to hear my station called halfway through proceedings. But it was Barbara, mother of comfort, calling that tea was ready. I washed my hands.

A strong smell of coal and a slice of homemade apple cake greeted us downstairs. Richard, who had stirred up the heater and boiled the kettle for tea, emerged from behind a curtained compartment in the kitchen, slightly blackened and smiling proudly. I glimpsed, before the curtain closed, an array of unfamiliar tools and a puzzling heavy, black, coal-consuming contraption about the size of an American washing machine. Barbara laid out her teacups and her visitor's book and her creased maps of Kudowa. Tea. At last something familiar. Breathing deeply, I could feel my whole self relaxing in the scent of it. Richard, who spoke Polish and not much at all, smiled; he had baked the cake and watched with pleasure our complete satisfaction at its consumption. Moist and crumbly, dusted with icing sugar, it was the best cake I had eaten in years.

Over that cake and tea, Barbara told us about the *Beinhaus*, about the local man who had gathered the bones and built it as a place of reconciliation, and about the Germans who had come back recently to repair it. Like ants that carry a weight of bread in heroic increments, they were there, working away by neighbourliness and generosity to purge a guilt that remained.

Too late by then to find the charnel house open, we settled for an evening stroll. Seizing a black showerproof shell of Barbara's from its peg in the hall, Richard thrust it in my direction. 'Take it,' he said in Polish, 'she will not mind. She is like Mother Mary, always thinking of someone else's comfort.' His face broke into a beaming smile, so proud of his simple, round, hospitable wife. The coat engulfed me, sleeves hiding my hands entirely, the pocket so low I had to bend over to find it. Like a child in her elder sister's cast-offs, I felt small and grateful in Barbara's coat.

We re-entered the damp twilight of beautiful, brutal Czermna, unsure of what we might find but calm in the knowledge that at least we had a bed for the night. Our first discovery was a small corner of the ossuary's courtyard dedicated to foreign graves – Hubert, Agnes, Ledwig, Karel, familien Kreigel, familien Aulich – Germans mostly and some Czechs, and a German/Polish plaque telling us that these women, men and children, whose homes were near Czermna and who now rested together in the designated plot, were reminding us of reconciliation.

Only steps away, across a cobbled courtyard, over the door of the chapel we had come to see, under the guardianship of two angels in the frieze overhead were carved in stone the words '*Kostnice, Kaplica Czaszek, Beinhaus*' – 'Ossuary', 'Skull Chapel' and 'Bone House', in Czech, Polish and German respectively. This area of land, so fought over, so tossed about, handed from victor to victor like a parcel, still seemed to defy the conventions of ownership. Shared by all these peoples, it was also home to all their dead.

As we cut back through the cemetery, evening mist rose over the hills, and we were taken out of our tiredness by the magic of dozens and dozens of flickering lights which glowed from as many graves. The dead were so much with us here, it was as if they had not ceased to be. 'Dozens of people', I said quietly, as Zuzana and I sat on the bench and listened, 'must have come here this evening from houses all over the village, and lit these.' I imagined their brief private pilgrimages from supper table to grave, from bus stop to cemetery gate. Had they spoken to each other, to their dead, to God?

How un-English, I thought – the monumental graves, the gravel underfoot, the cold metal benches and faded silk bouquets. The graves were mainly marble, shining as if varnished. They were feted with flowers and silk bouquets fresh and drooping, and some were planted up as gardens with roses and everlastings or with colourful busy lizzies, begonias, petunias. There were benches dotted randomly where one could sit and be friendly with one's earth-under family and with one's memories, with the sounds of evening as we were: mournful bullfinches calling to soundless batwings, cicadas clicking in a sleep-inducing drone.

Across the fields, squares of light appeared in farmhouses and cottages and then, as full night descended, a comfortable woman in a cardigan smiled at us as she closed up for the night. It was 9.30 p.m. Reluctantly we rose and left the night-lights in their lanterns burning yellow, green, orange, reddish, white, a village of prayers, or souls, or something I cannot name – presences – behind. In the morning they would have expired, I expected, or been extinguished.

There was no loneliness on that hillside but a steady falling stillness. Not approaching silence, pierced as it was by near birds and distant haloos of youths down in the town below, but quiet, as if the quieter you got inside the bigger your ears became. Here was the company of the dead and the company of the living (birds, boys, bugs) tumbling together like stones and water in a brook and creating out of the counterplay of their contrary motion and immobility a kind of music that was sometimes harmony and sometimes dissonance.

The tourist brochure calls this place a 'Sanktuarium Milczemia' – 'Sanctuary of Silence' – a noun made of a verb, like our English gerund; it implies active silence, a cessation of speech rather than the absence of sound. One didn't have to find words at all, just listen and watch. Watch the evening fall, houses disappearing into darkness, the lighted window squares appearing, candle lanterns flickering on graves; listen to a howl of a guard dog, the rising and falling churr of the nightjars, a chug of buses far away, the call of open spaces and finally, behind one's back, a clank of keys.

Back at the cottage, with too much inside my head, I drew a chair up to the crackling log fire and wrote until I felt the pen about to drop from my hands. Still I could not sleep until, well past midnight, Zuzana and I laughed ourselves to tears as we ran through all the absurdities of the day. Tears perhaps and laughter are what we needed, I think now, as I write these memories into a book. How else can any of us face mortality? The unexpected joys of life, the grim brutalities of death? Tears and laughter and friends.

Blind and slow as slugs, we rose next morning to find an enthusiastic note from Barbara. 'Halo girls,' it read, 'here is tee, coffe, pestry. Do not drink the weter.' Rummaging in the bursting cupboards for a saucepan, I found threescore of them stacked inside each other like Russian dolls and learned that Richard and Barbara do not live in a disposable world. Water boiled, I sank a nameless tea bag, stirred the coffee which floated in Zuzana's cup like sawdust. There was a small but ample jam-jar of milk, half of a half-squeezed lemon wrapped carefully in twice-used foil, two remaining pieces of Richard's apple cake and a generous jar of home-pickled cucumber slices.

I expected pickles with apple cake to make me feel almost as giddy as the cocktail of pictures upstairs had done; what I felt instead was a sense of gratitude. I had been given the best there was

– fruit of the ground and work of human hands. The frugality and generosity of this breakfast touched me deeply. Locking the door behind us and leaving the keys, we carried our bags from Barbara's a little sadly, orphans again in a sea of strangeness in search of the meaning of bones.

* * *

I had set out on this journey wanting to let myself be awakened by strangeness. I had thought this would mean having a mind like an empty book, with pristine pages, ready to record impressions. Certainly many impressions came – fast and furious and sometimes too many to process all at once. But there is another kind of innocence I did not know I had to find. It does not have primarily to do with spotlessness but with receptivity. It is not blank merely, but bright-faced and open. It deals not in the absence of impressions but in the willingness to receive them.

The stranger, like Traherne's infant, receives. Not only information, not only impressions or experiences or knowledge. He or she also receives degrees of brutality and kindness. The infant who does not receive kindness dies. Simple as that. The parameters of life and death that are stark for an infant may be less stark for adult strangers who have at least the wit, the mobility, the strength to feed themselves, seek shelter and defend themselves from attack. This journey never brought me to the brink of danger as other adventures have done, but it has taken me deeper into the knowledge of my need of other people, deeper into gratitude for kindnesses and deeper into an understanding of those simple things which are common to all humanity. It reminded me that need is sometimes the mother of receptivity.

I had chosen Barbara's house because it offered an authentic slice of local life, because it looked zany and fun and quirky. I had not thought about it belonging to someone who loved it and who might offer it without guile to strangers. We came in inquisitiveness, willing to be charmed by the naive. Equipped with a small knowledge of art and the benefit of some of the world's best galleries behind me, I came smiling and friendly, and with a secret sliver of superciliousness sharp as a scimitar, curved as a smile, stashed in the lining of my coat. It sneaked past all airport security; it sneaked past my best intentions. It was not until I saw it out of the corner of my eye flashing its keen edge in the direction of the plastic Smurf collection that stood on the top of Barbara's antiquated television that I was even aware it was there.

How do you rid yourself of such odiousness? How do you get the broom to reach the utmost corners of your heart? I was glad of Barbara's coat. Glad of its warmth. Grateful too to feel myself shrunken in its capaciousness, to be humbled by my need of it. Wearing it I began to understand the difference between curiosity and receptivity.

It was good to have had to travel a long way to our first charnel house; I had to be taken far away from the familiar. Hungry, worried, displaced, tired, faced with brutality and beauty, only then was I ready to see. How much it takes to have open eyes.

* * *

The Skull Chapel in Czermna was built in 1776, the year that Edward Gibbon's first volume of the *Decline and Fall of the Roman Empire* was published and Adam Smith was bringing to the world his *Wealth of Nations*; the same year that my home country the United States was being born. It was a leap year, with an erratic summer which saw unprecedented storms in New York. In July the Liberty Bell in Philadelphia rang for the first public reading of the *Declaration of Independence*, and Mozart's celebrated *Haffner*

Serenade was first performed in Salzburg, Austria – war being declared in one place while great music was being made in another.

That same summer, in a remote corner of what was then called Lower Silesia, the remnants of past wars were reasserting themselves for legend has it that, while the local parish priest Vaclav Tomaszek was out walking, the noses of his dogs discovered something new in the low-lying fields nearby. Bones. Human bones. Following the trail of his super-sentient dogs, he was horrified to discover feet and shoulders, elbows and ankles protruding in places between the bunches of long waving grass. Some of the bones had been clean clear of skin for a more than a hundred years; some of them had been dead hardly more than ten. These were the mass graves of victims of the Thirty Years' War (1618–48) and the more recent three Silesian Wars (1740–63). There were shallow graves too of people who had died of cholera epidemics and starvation that followed the wars. Too many bodies, too many wars. Too little respect afforded to these fallen.

One by one, so the tale goes, he started carrying the dead up from the shallow graves. Two of his fellow villagers, Schmidt and Langer, came with carts to help him. They worked through the whole hot summer, rags tied over their noses in the dust, skull after skull, bone after fractured bone, collecting up the toothless fragments of human life.

Another account suggests that a gathering of bones already existed in Czermna, in a wooden charnel house so dilapidated that dogs were able to enter, dig out the bones and carry them off; and that Vaclav Tomaszek's rebuilding and additions to it were aided by the parish gravedigger Josef Pfleger. Perhaps there is truth in both stories. He may have been aided by all three men and more as he took an inheritance of bones that had become prey to dogs – victims of wars and epidemics – and gathered, cleaned, restored and secured them in this huge project begun in that summer of 1776.

In October, from the opposite end of kingdoms to Czermna, from Stettin in the northwest corner of Poland by the Baltic Sea, the tall, buxom, seventeen-year old Sophie Marie Dorothea of Württemberg went to marry the crown Prince Paul of Russia. An intelligent, multilingual, rosy-cheeked young woman adored by all the court, she would become the Empress of Russia and mother of Tsars. While one European empire blossomed, in Britain the future looked bleak, for that same October, on All Hallows Eve in London, King George III admitted to Parliament that all was not going well for Britain in the war against the Americans. Quietly, as if immured from these international disputes and alliances, in Czermna, Vaclav Tomaszek sorted still more bones for the chapel that was being built. Three thousand skulls in the chapel above, a purported 21,000 more in its crypt.

It took him eighteen years to build the chapel, ten more to finish gathering, cleaning and arranging the bones. By the time he and his colleagues had finished in 1804, America, which had just declared war when he started, had gained its independence and was engaged in the business of becoming a nation, ratifying amendments to its constitution and, in the Louisiana Purchase, acquiring from France that vast tract of land that stretched from the mouth of the Mississippi through the Mid-West and all the way up to Canada. The northern states had abolished slavery and battle lines were being drawn up for the next (the Civil) war that would decimate its population.

During all of this time Vaclav Tomaszek is thought to have been bone-hunting, gathering up the scattered German bones and the Czech bones, the Polish bones and the Silesian bones. Bones of soldiers whose armies and sometimes whole nations had long ago disappeared, and bones of the women they raped and sometimes the women they loved. In 1804 in England, William Pitt the

Younger began his second term as Prime Minister, while in Paris Napoleon Bonaparte crowned himself the first Emperor of France. As far off as Haiti, in the only successful slave revolt ever, Haitians gained their independence from France, while Serbia began its revolt from the Ottoman Empire.

As the world turned radically around him, Vaclav Tomaszek completed his single-minded task. Clawing order from an inherited chaos, he gathered up the broken bits of anonymous humans, cleaned and stored the unclaimed remains. A frieze was carved on the outside of the chapel above the doorway: two handsome angels reclining on either side of a skull and crossbones. One held a chalice, the other an hourglass. Above them all, he had carved a triangle with an all-seeing eye ever-open in its centre – symbol of the Holy Trinity and the ever-watchful eye of God. When all the 24,000 were in their final resting place and his job was finished, he fastened the shutters. There were stone walls in carved Baroque and a pantile roof. Never again would dogs be able to find them.

* * *

This is how it is inside. Solid walls of skulls and femurs rise to a ceiling heavily hung with skulls and crossbones suspended on wires. You cannot avert your eyes; there is nowhere the bones are not, and many of them at hand height are polished to an impossibly shiny black with touching. It is a small room. One coachload of people standing shoulder to shoulder fills it entirely, and Zuzana and I are pushed by shuffling schoolchildren to the very edges, right to the walls, so that my legs are touching those polished femurs, my shoulder a skull's cheek. If I were to turn my head even slightly to the left my eye would look straight into an empty socket, my nose would probably fit neatly into the triangular gap where its nose had been. It would, lipless, kiss me.

Plank-stiff I freeze, keep my eyes on Sister Maria of the microphone whose mouth intones in weary Polish the story of the *Kapila
Czaszek*. The unfamiliar vowels tell me nothing except that she is
bored; the skull perched just whispering distance from my ear tells
me not to move an inch. I don't. Sister Maria points to the bones
above, around her and below. Moving my eyeballs only, I glance up
at the ceiling; see there, in the crossbones and skulls, the warning
for piracy and poison, repeated over and over again like an incan-
tation: 'herein death, death herein'.

On one side of the chapel, in a niche half-obscured by protruding
femurs, stands a sculpture of the messenger angel Gabriel who was
sent to announce the conception of Christ to the Virgin Mary. A
gilded band wraps round his muscular bicep and in his left hand
he holds a trumpet, as you might expect a heavenly herald to do.
'Raise the dead', the inscription on his niche proclaims. Opposite
him in a similar niche another angel, the archangel Michael, famous
in battle, holds a balancing scale. 'Come to court', he calls. Life and
judgment are coupled here – there is no hope of one without the
other; the day of resurrection is also the day of reckoning. To be
awake is to bear the consequences of one's actions.

I know this charnel house is meant to be a place of reconciliation,
that the bones of victim and perpetrator alike have been gathered,
the vanquished and the victors laid side by side regardless of race
or station. In this place beyond speech, where linguistic differences can have no bearing on their fellowship, it cannot matter that
German and Pole and Czech and old Silesian mingle indetermi-
nately. Common humanity, the dignity of all is what I am meant to
sense, but all I feel is difference, hostility.

At the east end, behind a marbled green, lace-dressed altar, skulls
alone are stacked floor to ceiling, each jawless chin seeming to devour
the ash-white cranium on which it rests. Of course this is nonsense;

skulls do nothing, least of all eat. The hostility I feel can only be coming from within me. And yet the walls of skulls are far too close for my liking. Stack them here and say their differences are somehow reconciled if you will, but their difference to me is certainly not.

Without moving my head, my eyes glance sideways at shoulder-skull. There are two remaining teeth in its unfortunate maxilla. They seem extraordinarily long. I am glad there is a vast chasm between the living and the dead. As if to ward off a gruesome nibble from those teeth, I remind myself of that chasm again and again while shoulder-skull bides his time four inches from my cheek.

There is fumbling at the front as weary Sister Maria swaps the microphone for specimen femurs: a broken and mended one, and the prize one of all, the long femur of a 2-metre man – 'a seventeenth-century giant', Zuzana whispers in translation. I am glad for this quirky diversion; so are the schoolchildren. Compelled by curiosity, they cease their fidgeting and their attempts at illicit skull-touching for a moment and listen. Laying on the altar beneath the painted and gilded crucifix is a display of skulls of particular interest: a mayor of Czermna and his wife, a skull eaten into lacy tracery by syphilis, the femur of a Tartar warrior and, of course, the skull of Vaclav Tomaszek himself who, after his labours were ended, came to join his friends.

The Polish word *czaszek*, says Sister Maria, is related to the Russian *chashka* or cup because the upside-down skull looks like a kind of cup. I am fascinated by this. It takes me away from my nervy gut and into my head, where I recall an article I read about the world's earliest human skull cups, recently discovered in Gough's Cave near Cheddar Gorge in Somerset. No one knows exactly what the Cro-Magnon cups were used for but they show signs of crafting (a euphemism for the tooth marks made by human gnawing) that correspond to primitive cups made in other parts of the world.

I remember related writings about Tibetan skull cups or *kapala* in Sanskrit: highly decorated ceremonial goblets, used in Tibetan Buddhist and in Hindu ritual for the oblation of wrathful deities, in which the history of the cranium's original owner has a bearing on its tantric potency. Skulls of children, virgins and murder victims being the most potent, a murdered child virgin was best. And accounts from many other places – from China where, in 177 BC, the son of a chieftain is reputed to have killed his king and made a drinking cup from his skull which became the blood-drinking cup for sealing a treaty. The fifth-century Greek historian Herodotus tells how the Scythians drank from the skulls of their enemies. In 1510, in what is now Uzbekistan, Shah Ismail I defeated Muhammad Shaybani and had his skull coated in gold and jewelled as a goblet. In the same century the Japanese warlord Oda Nobunaga took the skulls of his enemies and had them used as *sake* cups, lacquered and covered in gold leaf.

Skull cups were not always trophies; sometimes they were tributes. The *Primary Chronicle* tells how the skull of Svyatoslav I of Kiev was made into a goblet from which the ruler's wife drank, praying for a son as brave as the deceased warlord. In England, 14,700 years after the tooth-gnawed Cheddar Gorge skull cups, nineteenth-century Lord Byron retrieved a skull found by his gardener, had it polished till it shone like tortoiseshell, and used it as a drinking cup. Claret was passed around, recalls Byron, 'whilst many a grim joke was cut at its expense'. He even made a poem about it.

I am just about to file the whole scary skull thing neatly in this gruesome but distantly academic archaeological skull/cup folder when the nun lays a cut-in-half one on the altar. It looks for all the world like a very primitive chalice. A chalice of what, I wonder. Suffering? Remembrance? Affinity? Reconciliation? Suddenly it is not just Vaclav Tomaszek's effort that is represented there, but mine too: all of those things remembered, lingering and unresolved. Dark as treacle, the unreconciled parts of my life have been poured into that primitive skull cup.

'Take this and drink' – the words of the liturgy echo in my warm and brain-sheltering skull. But I do not want to. I do not even want to stand here in this small death-crowded room one more minute. I have not travelled a thousand miles into foreign lands in order to tease the tangles of a lifetime. I have simply come to investigate interesting facts. 'Look at Sister Maria', suggests shoulder-skull. She is pointing to the skull of a woman with a hole in her head who has stopped remembering but is still reminding us of battles military and domestic.

Stranger than strange are these walls of the dead. They have no place speaking to me. I have come here to beat fear. I have set out to overcome, to be fearless and victorious, not alien and intimidated. But I see already that it will not be as simple as that. I cannot escape the alien, not only because in Czermna I am a foreigner, staying in a deeply idiosyncratic and random house. Those oddities are just the precursors to the Strangeness with a capital 'S' that we find in death. I knew before I set out that it was weird to share your house with hundreds of skeletons, and that a tour of ossuaries was not your typical holiday but, standing here with a skull whispering in my ear, I see that this tour of bones is alien in its very essence. Its destinations mark the proximity and inevitability of death, unavoidably and characteristically a place of alienation, whose farewell is not merely a buoyant *bon voyage*. You go into the absolute unknown, leaving behind everyone you love, everything you know, even your flesh and bones.

What I just begin to see, like a flicker at the edge of my field of vision, as I stand in that charnel house, is that it is quite possible

I shall not slay this fear at all and that what is being offered to me is a chance for a different kind of victory. Not to silence these odd and disturbing bones, but to embrace them. How are you dealing with the broken bits, the small and large estrangements in your life? they ask. In this place of reconciliation I am not reconciled to my mortality and I know that there are lost and broken parts of my life that still lie as scattered as Vaclav Tomaszek's bones.

When the double doors open I am as eager as the children are to burst out into open space and fresh air. I wonder if they have encountered mortality as I have, the sense that life is brief and that there is a house to put in order. Boisterous and bouncing, they collide with the next large school group waiting to enter. There is a long queue and they will be packed in to capacity. Another coachload will follow. I ask the children what they thought of the chapel. They shrug; it was part of an exciting day out, out of the ordinary but not momentous. 'Do you want the same thing to happen to your skull?' I ask. 'No, no!' they cry in unison. 'Are you scared of being like that one day – just bones?' 'No,' they say smiling, 'we are not scared to die.' This afternoon they will go from the bone house to the high-level ropes course in the woods beyond Kudowa to test the limits of their courage. Then they will go for an ice cream at the spa. Death, daring and delight will pound the walls of their dreams tonight like unleashed squash balls.

After the children had gone and the square was empty and quiet, I turned back. Easier here, on the outside, in the open air, I took one last look at the exterior of the small neat chapel, its smooth creamy stucco walls, its solid doors, its sky-high angels offering sacrament and memento. Handsome and young, they sit forever with perfect posture, wings proud, faces calm, Silesian breezes gently blowing their hair. Strong and flawless, they would outlive us all.

That is what the bones said, too, that lay carved between them, skull over bare crossbones. The trilingual inscription 'Kostnice, *Kaplica Czaszek, Beinhaus*' was meant to name what lies behind its doors. Looking again at a photo of the chapel pinned to the notice-board by my desk, I see that in fact no words are needed. Whatever your mother tongue, you can tell just from looking at the frieze what you will find inside: a chalice of wine and the passage of time and bones guarded by angels under the all-seeing eye of God. I do not doubt that Vaclav Tomaszek felt himself to be under that eye when he carried out his long and demanding labours. I imagine it was not merely an overbearing love of tidiness that compelled him to embark on his task, but a greater longing to return something lost, redeem something damned; to restore human dignity.

Even with that task complete, the Skull Chapel at Czermna continues to function as a place where the stain of war may be expunged. I recalled Barbara's story from the previous evening about expelled twentieth-century Germans and of the twenty-first-century ones who came back a few years ago to repair the floor of the *Beinhaus* that was falling in.

* * *

When I think about the Czermna charnel house now it does not fill me with fear. From the distance of my keyboard and my screen there almost seems to be something tamed about it, as if the efforts of Vaclav Tomaszek to claw order out of chaos were like the long labours of a lion trainer. He, quietly persistent and determined, pitting his patience against death's as if it were a weapon. He could not win, of course, but he did manage to state clearly something about human dignity, a message that derives not from some great act of valour on his part but from the extraordinary respect he paid to the ordinary. Nothing, after all, is more ordinary than our bones.

Without our skin and hair, our eyes and teeth, we look pretty much the same whoever we are, wherever we come from. It almost doesn't matter to whom the bones belong – they could be anyone's.

Czermna itself seems to me a place that does not know to whom it belongs. Passing from the hands of one ruler to another, through religious and irreligious regimes, having no mother tongue but change, it carries the imprint of Germanic, Slavonic, Lechitic languages in the engravings on its tombstones like hieroglyphs. If there is one language spoken in the Czermna charnel house it is the language of beloved dust – all of us coming up from dust, returning slowly to it in a regular rhythm of human mortality. Even the shape of the bones is mainly regular – so regular, in fact, that skulls and femurs can be stacked with something near the precision of bricks. 'Each of these more or less samenesses matters', is what Vaclav's endeavours say.

The bones are not here distinguished by race, language, nationality, sex – the features that, while living, shaped their lives and often their deaths. A few particularly curious skulls are singled out, but the thousands that line the walls and ceiling, and that lie in piles below, say simply this: the ordinary matters. A life, however unspectacular, however unremarkable, however simple, is after all a human life and worthy of respect just because it is.

It was not only to these dead that Vaclav rendered respect in making that claim; he rendered it to his life too. Generations and an ocean away, he rendered it to my life and to yours. No life should be discarded, he said, spade after earth-filled spade. The diseased and the lame, the old, the broken, the full and the pregnant, the lusty and the lean, the soldiers with arms of chiselled strength mown down at the height of their power. They are all here, in his charnel house. Every human qualifies. Even enemies. No, I mean, especially enemies; the very fact that there were so many generations of enmity is part of what generated the need for this charnel house in the first place. I feel encouraged by the work of reconciliation that was done here and by the fact that even today it remains a place where those who seek to repair the damage of the past may find a way to do so.

And now, months after my journey I begin to understand that the link between strangeness and forgiveness that was first suggested to me in that charnel house in Czermna is a deeper one than I had thought. When you embrace the stranger you make your enemy your friend. It is not just that travelling to unfamiliar places, becoming for some brief time a sojourner and an innocent, may open one's mind to learning, though that is true. There is a stranger also at your gate. Although at the time I was not able to respond to that challenge, Czermna's question – Are the broken parts of your deep self being healed? – has haunted me. And I sense that deep healing and embracing the stranger are linked.

The bones in my cellar are my neighbours by proximity but not yet neighbours of my heart. I think of the admonition to 'love your neighbour as yourself' that was once spoken by Jesus of Nazareth, perhaps the most familiar of all stories about how we might react to a stranger – the story of the Good Samaritan. A man was walking along a road and he was set upon by thieves who beat him and robbed him and left him to die. It is a story that offers no excuses to the self-righteous and stands expectation on its head, because it is the 'friend' who passes the injured man by and the despised rival who befriends. Healing and forgiveness go hand in hand with this embracing of the stranger.

Who is my neighbour? My newest neighbours are going to be bones; and I have been invited to embrace the bones within, to 'count my days', as the Psalmist says, because looking at mortality can make you wise. I see that now. But then, as I prepared to leave the site of our first charnel house, what I carried was a sack of jumbled impressions, a sense of alienation and sweet memories of kindness received.

*   *   *

On the bus leaving Kudowa I gathered my bags and sought to arrange my disjointed thoughts. I tried to make some kind of sense of the things I had seen and witnessed: the faded charm of Kudowa, its natural beauty and the full-hearted generosity of Barbara and Richard, their zany art collection with its yearning to give the irrepressible human spirit an airing. The struggle they and their neighbours have had for generations to stay alive through hard times. A warm coat offered to a stranger, and a man bloodied red in the street – that startling cocktail of kindness and brutality that is still, perhaps always, just beneath the surface of our everyday lives. I mulled over the linguistic and littoral legacy of battle: place names that change with victors, and bleached bones like beached driftwood protruding from the shore of a past war. I remembered walls of skulls and the joint of a giant. Bare bones and mineral springs. The things that remain.

The water does not change. Though the name of the place changes, victors change and with them languages, customs, laws, the water at Kudowa has remained its mineral self – ecologically purified and full of iron, useful for stimulating the metabolism and thereby treating circulatory ailments, heart valve defects, murmurs, endocrine system illnesses such as hyperactive thyroid, obesity, migraines and rheumatism.

With mineral integrity, while the world changed radically around him, Vaclav Tomaszek stayed true and fulfilled his single-minded task. Though no one understands them, Barbara and Richard maintain their quietly eccentric and artistic endeavours. I do not know whether it is owing to accident or precedent that these curious acts of collection and reconciliation have occurred in an ancient place of healing. Barbara's collected objects appear to bear no relation to each other. They coexist, portrait alongside beer bottle alongside saucepans and lace and blackening coal-fired boiler. Vaclav's intention is deliberate; reconciliation his clearly stated aim.

Both of them collectors of fragments, valuers of the lost and discarded, their collections rise indiscriminately from cultures not by being selected but by being gathered. We are so used to choice, our days a succession of selections, as if it is only by exercising our power to choose that we know we exist. Both Barbara and Vaclav Tomaszek gathered everything up, discarded nothing, believing that even the merest object could be redeemed – indeed, perhaps, that without the merest object nothing was redeemed. For Barbara it is usefulness that ascribes value, whereas for Vaclav simple humanity is value enough, and yet redemption is their common theme. Inclusion is their method.

This is almost the opposite to what I have come to understand about worthwhile activity. Trained in the deductive method of reasoning, educated to within a whisker of my ability to enjoy that education, my mind has been shaped to discriminate, to weigh, value, toss aside the inessential, jettison the irrelevant. Indeed, it has been shaped in such a way that only when discarding can it be certain it is on the path to clarity. It is only by reducing ideas or beliefs to their bare essentials that one can get at a kernel of truth. There is a certain valuable fruit at the end of this process. But there is a different fruit at the end of theirs, one I have not often tasted. I am not sure how I can carry any of it home with me without it spoiling on the way.

I wanted to stay a little longer in Czermna, to linger with these little-known and unmarked histories. I wanted to understand a fraction of the turmoil of this place and its deep need for peace; to drink its waters and let my sweet-coursing blood be pleased. Sad at our swift departing, I watched the town's houses and parochial shops pass by and then, suddenly, alongside the road there was a dog remarkably like Barbara's, and a man standing next to the dog seeming to point to it meaningfully. It was Richard, smiling serenely, and he was not pointing at the dog at all but beyond it to Barbara, whose big heart had pushed her body across a lane of traffic to stand in the median, in her borrowed jumper and her shining smile, waving with unabashed affection at two halo girls in a passing yellow bus.

3

Sedlec

Leaving behind the remote bone chapel at Czermna in Poland, we headed 110 kilometres south and west by train to the Czech Republic and its famous ossuary at Sedlec in Kutna Hora. The photographs of Sedlec with its bone chandeliers and skull pyramids were so gruesome and ghoulish that I expected this charnel house to be the somewhat spooky highlight of our tour of weird wonders. It is a place, we were to discover, where legend and history meet. New meanings emerge in each generation, so that what the bones meant then and to those people are not necessarily what they mean now and to me, or to you.

Or then again, maybe in some sense they are – because, within the contradictions at Sedlec brought about by the evolution of the monastery, its destruction, restoration, the accretion of bones, the conflicting architectural and artistic transitions it underwent, and the advent of modern tourism, a thread remains that has to do with resurrection. And that has to do with the inescapable contrasting demands of transformation and continuity and, finally, with what we humans mean by hope.

Our first stop was Sedlec's cathedral and our first storyteller Jiří Arnet, hospitable and smiling in neat trousers and an ironed shirt, a guide whose excellent English was matched by an extensive knowledge of the place and its history. For the Sedlec story starts long before its charnel house.

It was 1142. The Cistercians were on the move; decades before, a restless monk known as Robert of Molesme, son of a French nobleman, had left his community to live with some hermits in small huts made of branches. For him the Benedictine life in traditional monasteries had become too comfortable and he wanted to return to a stricter interpretation of St Benedict's Rule. He and the hermits found this austerity at Molesme with their stick huts and a chapel dedicated to the Holy Trinity in the woods but, as Robert's reputation for sanctity grew, so did Molesme, and it became wealthier, and its practice became lax. So Robert left again to found another new monastery in a desolate valley deep within the forest at Citeaux, near Dijon in eastern France, in 1098. They were the first Cistercians.

Casting off their black Benedictine habits and donning a new white habit and black scapula (or apron), these first Cistercians made plain their wish to simplify. Cluny, the Benedictine monastery from which Robert of Molesme had come, was one of the most powerful in the history of Europe. In fact, it was more than a monastery; it was a whole network of communities, with Cluniac houses not only in France but in England too – in Lewes in Sussex, and Much Wenlock in Shropshire, and Castle Acre in Norfolk – and its wealth was legendary.

It was this wealth to which Robert of Molesme objected when he went to live in his hut of sticks. He was not alone; the Cistercian movement gained many followers. By the end of the twelfth century there were Cistercian houses spread throughout France and into England, Wales, Scotland, Ireland, Spain, Portugal, Italy and Eastern Europe. Among them was the house at Sedlec. So, right from the start, it seems that Sedlec was about simplicity. And not just the easy or accidental simplicity of a daisy or a child; rather that deliberate simplicity that results from paring down and casting off. Simplicity excavated from the rocks of ambition.

Even if you know nothing of how the Cistercians came to be, nothing of their reforming zeal and their simplicity, in Sedlec Cathedral you feel the open space their austerity created. The unadorned cathedral with its creamy limewashed walls and clear windows admitting great swathes of light, with its bare stone floors and spare furnishings, invites tranquillity. Not just to your eyes, but to your mind and even to your lungs. You take a deep breath, exhale it slowly, breathe again. The cathedral breathes with you, easily, the great surging pillars extending down its nave at once rooted and straight as a row of ancient, elegiac elms.

Present in these stones are the praises and lamentations of generations. Cistercian simplicity and sufficiency are embodied here, not concepts merely, nor even rules of life, but physical realities in stone arches at once humble and soaring. Looking between those arches into the north transept you can see cunningly crafted self-supporting stone steps spiralling upward in airy flight, curled as the paring of a carpenter's plane, marvellous as a DNA molecule.

I think of how fascinated we are in the modern age with DNA, the secrets it unlocks – history, identity, biological inheritance – suggesting strengths and susceptibilities to our twenty-first-century consciousnesses as fortune tellers might have done to our forebears. We look back to discover our belonging and look forward to predict or circumvent our fates, our scientific sorceress the millionth magnification of a microscope, its thin slides uplifting totemic drops of blood, saliva-stained fibres, a plucked hair. Sedlec's charnel house is heaped with such DNA. But it seems to me there is another kind of DNA in the place, not specific to individuals: deep, inherited, identifying features that are corporately shared and reside not only in the charnel house full of bones, but also metaphorically in the stories told by the charnel house and its cathedral. Here in these formative pasts we catch a glimpse of the continuing nature of the place; we see part of the cultural DNA, if you like, of Bohemia, where destruction and restoration seem perpetually to chase each other's tails.

Built, as we know, by the Cistercians in the twelfth century, the cathedral of Our Lady and St John the Baptist was plundered by the Hussites in 1421. It was restored in 1709 only to become a state tobacco barn a hundred years later in 1812. Now a UNESCO World Heritage Site, it has been restored yet again with great care and sensitivity, a monument to the beauty of light, stone, wood and faithfulness.

Down the north side of the nave runs a series of enormous twenty-foot canvasses depicting scenes from this resurrection history. Our guide Jiří points to the first: a man on a horse and other men, in white robes; there are trees and animals and a whole sylvan landscape to scan, before the eye is eventually drawn to the figures at the centre giving and receiving something ... one small box – a doll's house? a dog house? a chest? It is the landowner and courtier Miroslav's donation to the Cistercians: the grant of land for the foundation of the monastery depicted in the model of a building handed over. And there is Abbot Heidenreich, friend of Wenceslas II, who had the first cathedral built. Good King Wenceslas, hitherto snowbound, suddenly leaps from a Christmas carol, has a summertime life and a purpose beyond his gift to the poor man on the feast of Stephen, in deep snow, crisp and even.

On another enormous canvas, fierce men with merciless swords and righteous zeal are slaying the swordless monks. Gruesome and gory, there is fire in the eyes of the triumphant and the dying alike. These warriors, Jiří tells us, are the Protestant Hussites, and we learn about the Hussite Wars, with the screaming of fleeing women, masculine skulls cracked open, entrails pinned to trees.

Centuries later there is the story of the dashing young architect Santini who at 25 designed the restored cathedral, spawning a whole genre called Gothic Baroque. Then bleak black-and-white photographs of the dry tobacco years, the dereliction of neglect. This was not just the history of a cathedral but a story of a nation, or a people – nations, really, and peoples, to be more correct – for this place was Bohemia and Austria-Hungary; it was Přemyslid and Hapsburg; it was Czechoslovakia; a protectorate of Germany; Soviet Communist and now, by a velvet revolution, a democratic capitalist republic. It was all of these things and none of them for none of them alone describes it entirely. I was standing in a place where history felt somehow not clearly linear but kaleidoscopic. Every time you turned the lens, different shapes and colours dropped into view and a whole new pattern emerged.

Intrigued, we left the cathedral and headed for the charnel house. It would take years to begin to know such a place, I reflected, as we walked from the cathedral of St Mary across a city road and up the easy ossuary hill, but at least we had some bare bones of Bohemian history on which to hang impressions as we encountered the human bones that were waiting. Those ossuary bones that had leapt as impossible monstrosities from the photographic files of the curious macabre to horrify and fascinate my disbelieving eyes; that had filled my shoes with question marks.

* * *

Up the hill as we approach, the ossuary at Sedlec looks like a small gothic church, buttresses at the west face and the north and south sides, long lancet windows, copper-topped towers. Its top half, All Saints Chapel, is light and bright, with space for prayer and an exhibition of photographs that aim to capture the play of light on stone, but visitors do not come for this; they come for the shocking human bones that lie below. Down the wide, steep stairs in the vaulted ossuary, massed in vast pyramids that reach to the ceiling, stacked, glued into sculptures, strung from the arches like garlands are the remains of some 40,000 persons, mainly victims of medieval plagues and the Hussite Wars. It is a spectacle most bizarre – compelling and revolting in equal measure.

The ossuary, started in 1400 and continued in 1511, is constructed on three levels. The entrance extension at ground level, designed (1703–10) by the same young Santini who restored the cathedral, feels somehow familiar; then immediately inside you must make a choice. Either you go down into gloomy half-light or you go up to the light chapel above. Descent was my intention and I did not linger for long over the trinket stall selling plastic skulls and luminous skeletons, but moved purposefully on.

The stairs were disconcertingly broad. Each could probably have accommodated ten people standing shoulder to shoulder, and there must have been 20 stairs. If they marched in military precision as do ants, two hundred people could descend all at once; these were stairs fit for a large influx of humanity. The descent was steep as well as wide, and for a moment I felt as if I might be swallowed. Zuzana and I paused, each as if to let the other go first, though in truth there was no need to pause; we had arrived near closing time, the place was empty, the steps could easily accommodate us side by side, and I realized the pause was not about courtesy at all. But still my feet would not budge. 'Shall we go down?' I asked Zuzana, who was also inexplicably waiting and, leaning slightly nearer to each other, we set out in the depressions worn smooth by the generations of footfalls that had preceded us.

* * *

The descent is swift; because it is also deep you cannot see much of the charnel house before you arrive in it, but you can feel the gradual temperature change almost immediately. There are bones mounted on the stone walls of the staircase, saying something, in pictures. Saying what? – fourteen inches from my face, near enough to be heard as a shout, but I cannot discern what they are saying. I see only a smattering of bones, intriguing and horrible, and the problem is not merely visual. The great 'what *is* this?' that I feel does not spring merely from an inability to read, but from a more fundamental question about how I am to regard the objects that face me. Are these bones artist's materials or human remains? And the 'what are they?' has triggered an as yet undescried 'what am I?' which has rendered me inexplicably and deeply unsettled.

Sublimating the inarticulate, I concentrate on looking. Gradually, my eyes decipher the bone symbols: a five-foot-tall chalice; the signature of František Rint (1870) the bone artist; the large Christian symbol IHS *Jesus Hominis Salvator* – Jesus, Saviour of mankind; and each recognition of a symbol or a name seems a small achievement. Or maybe what I sense is simply relief that what I first saw as a human thigh, a finger, a shoulder blade and a few ivory ribs I can now see as a picture. I do not want to see the individual fingers, ribs, femur, scapula; I do not want to think about where they came from. My stomach rights itself again. As artist's materials they are so much less personal and particular.

Descending to the last step, my hand firmly gripping the railing, I focus on the symbols and try very hard to resist mentally unpicking the parts. I try to tell myself that this is art and see it whole, but I do not entirely succeed. High on a stone pedestal flanked by columns of stacked skulls and femurs, eight pelvises line up to form the curve of a giant bone chalice. Knobbly ends of femurs and lacy sacrum shields splay against the flat planes of pelvises as the chalice curves towards its thin fibia stem. What giant hand would hold this blood cup? What kind of wine is poured from someone else's pelvis? Still gripping the railing, I descend further.

My feet hit the simple stone of the charnel house floor. In front of me at the foot of the stairs, four thin towers of skulls and bones, about ten feet tall, stand like pillars in the short central hall beyond which, at the far end of the charnel house, is a chapel on whose walls are mounted further bone decorations: a huge bone monstrance, a bone wreath. The altar in this chapel is simple and bare and at its feet lay small piles of disconnected bones. High in the arches before and alongside the chapel, ropes of skulls are hung as if they were festive garlands, cranial curves and edges like fists of roses or clumps of chrysanthemums, a bizarre harvest from some garden of the dead.

Over the four towers is suspended, like a spook's corona, what is perhaps Rint's *pièce de résistance*: an enormous bone chandelier reputed to contain (many times over) every one of the two hundred and six bones in the human body. The chandelier hangs so near the four towers of bones that looking up all is bone. Bone above me, bone around me, bone beside me, bone before me; thousands of disjointed bones orchestrated, prized and pieced, punctuated by the dark vacancies of socket and jaw.

I shudder. I keep my hands from covering my ears, because they want to shut out all this discord, though the noise is actually inside me – bones in mid-air suspended, flying bones that should still be lying companionably with their fellows. Wanting to run out from under these fitful bones, away from this restless cacophony, I make myself stand here, under and amid it. I stand and look.

I notice, as if belonging to some other hopeful realm, small lights glimmering at the chandelier's tips. Breathing slowly, calmly, I spy among the many shades of ivory, stone and ash of the bones, glimmering gilded wings, harbingers of life. And then I see that these belong to four rubicund painted plaster cherubs, one atop each of the four thin towers. The cheeks of the one nearest me are plumped out with breath as he presses the air into his trumpet; on his peachy knee sits a human skull, his tinted hand shiny and bright against the chalky grey cranium. His sheer fleshiness seems a delight to my bone-dried eyes. I can almost feel the air that fills his cheeks. I wonder what he is announcing with such petulance. And then I am glad of his petulance, for it means he looks alive enough to have a mood.

Away from these disconcerting concoctions, in the farthest four corners of the charnel house or *kostnice*, corresponding to the combined points of the compass, NE, NW, SE, SW, stand four large rounded pyramids of skulls over each of which is suspended a gilded coronet. In each, the solid mass of skulls has been tunnelled through and lit from inside with electric lights to give a sense of their great depth and proportions.

Each mound is locked behind wood and metalwork screens that fill the space from the floor up to the overhead arches. Nevertheless, generations of visitors have tried to reach them. Here and there the perfect balance of skull on skull has been jarred by some rogue's reach, the screening breached by a daredevil's bravado. Many skulls have coins in their eye sockets or between their jaws. Well-wishers, perhaps, seeking good luck; lovers maybe with a wish on their lips; gamblers hoping for a lucky toss. Or maybe those glinting coins signify an unthought instinct to pacify the dead lest the dead seek retribution for the disturbances we bring.

There is little rest, it seems to me, for these remains. I am disquieted by the bone plaques and chalices, the dismembering that they reiterate, the frippery of skull garlands, the jocular tilt of the chandelier. There is something subversive in these that offends the sense of decency in me; perhaps one of the points of art is to subvert and disturb 'normal', but I find them contrived and offputting. The simple mounds of skulls, however, draw me back to look at them again. Despite the chancy glint of coins there is something solemn and beautiful about them. The skulls neither reject nor receive these mementoes; the intentions of visitors move them not one iota. They simply stare out in all directions in unbroken silence. Some people say the shapes are not pyramids but bells. In Slovak, Zuzana tells me, tolling bells are thought to be God's voice. Maybe they are bells calling to prayer. They could just as well be tolling the death knell for us all.

I think it is the sheer number of skulls in those mounds that moves me. If they have a voice, this is it: a voice of solidarity. Whether that is a solidarity of the dead or of all human beings I cannot tell. Fingers curled around the cool ironwork screen, I lean my face against the wooden bars, peer at one skull after another, looking for some clue, for individuality perhaps, for some identifying feature that might suggest a story. There are hundreds of minute differences between them, but the overall effect is unity. Except for the Hussite warriors in the glass museum case at the foot of the stairs, whose skulls showed the blows of blades – one even bearing a fault line cracked and re-grown – the skulls here, particularly the mountains of skulls, tell no personal tales. Whatever their lives, there is now only one story they share. Together they wait.

* * *

Legend has it that in 1278 the Cistercian Abbot Henry brought back with him from the Holy Land a handful of soil, given by the King of Jerusalem, which he sprinkled on the cemetery at Sedlec, making it hallowed ground. The ground itself was believed to have special properties that could rot the body swiftly, thus releasing the soul to

Paradise. This theory spawned a myth that burial at Sedlec would guarantee a place in heaven within three days of death. We are told that people journeyed from many parts of medieval Europe to be buried there, travelling in great discomfort, or carried in carts over rough roads by their families as death approached.

In the end too many people came to be buried in Sedlec. First the legend of quick release made Sedlec the favoured burial spot with Central Europe's elite; then the plagues of the fourteenth century and the Hussite Wars of the fifteenth decimated the population. Old remains were exhumed to make way for new burials, and bones piled up in churches.

The first skull pyramid, they say, was constructed by a half-blind Cistercian who was given the task of collecting up these exhumed remains. He started making order out of chaos, one skull at a time. Centuries and renovations later, we see the result of the work he began. Skull after skull placed with complete anonymity and respectful carefulness, one alongside the other, over and over again, stacked row upon row, until together they make a pyramid of human loss both horrifying and beautiful. There are thousands and thousands of unrelated persons pressed into intimate proximity approximating to a familiarity they can scarce have known. Eyeless sockets, unblinking, tell the brutal truth of their mortality and mine. Whether one regards these skulls as fellows or merely as bricks in a wall, their stories come to this – a common humanity, the brevity of life, the longevity of bones and, for the ones who put them here, the hope of resurrection.

Resurrection is a hope that I feel Western society has mainly lost. At the very least it is a hope about which we know little, and so about which we hardly dare speak with conviction. The large numbers of resolved atheists who might see resurrection as complete nonsense, and the even larger number of agnostics who thrive on a healthy dose of doubt, are not the only ones who may feel that resurrectionists are on wobbly ground. Believers too, of many kinds, have little idea what resurrection life might be like. I use the term 'believer' here in the broadest possible sense – the very many people who, deep down, cannot convince themselves that death is the utter end; who believe that life goes on but are not sure whether they think that will be a resurrection, or a reincarnation, or a kind of ghostly lingering.

Among those believers are the millions who would call themselves Christians, who would expect a resurrection and would look to Scripture for an indication about what that might look like. But even here the details are few. There is the story of the poor man Lazarus in an afterlife and the rich man in suffering who asks if Lazarus might dip his finger in water and give the rich man a drop. Whole essays have been written on the degree to which this suggests that bodies with fingers are real in post-mortem life.

Then there are the accounts of Jesus' actions after his resurrection in which he seems to do very ordinary and physical things – walking and talking, cooking and eating – and in which he does extraordinary things like appearing in a locked room, or walking on water, or ascending into heaven. These passages of Scripture suggest that resurrection bodies are real, physical bodies capable of speech and digestion, but not exactly like the bodies we have now. Apart from these examples, there is not much in the way of specific description of the resurrection life in the Christian scriptures.

Standing looking at those hills of skulls in Sedlec, I realize that I have been surrounded by a landscape of Christianity for years and yet I know little about how the ideas surrounding its core belief of resurrection evolved. Thoughtful, with those solemn skull mounds behind me, I mount the stairs, through layers of cold and up towards the heavy wooden charnel house door which stands ajar, admitting a warm yellow shaft of low, late afternoon light.

* * *

In a medieval stone house across the road from the charnel house I met Karel Koubsky (42) who, as the ossuary's first twenty-first-century administrator, has the peculiar task of maintaining the chapel and ensuring its future. It is a job he never expected to have, although he grew up as familiar with the ossuary as anyone could be: his father was administrator before him. He likes his job. 'I should have done it earlier', he says, but it was a challenge he did not want to meet when he was younger and went off to work as a computer programmer.

As a teenager the ossuary was a place of thrills; he and some friends once dared each other to spend the night there. Now it is both a business and a vocation to him. He is interested in how the place affects its visitors; he has seen so many people arrive noisy and gradually calm down. Sometimes companies hire the ossuary after hours for corporate hospitality. Almost invariably, Karel says, there is someone among these professional persons for whom the experience is overwhelming. 'There is something you can't explain about this place,' he confesses, 'it opens people up.' He has seen the hardest-looking people, punks covered in tattoos and piercings, arrive edgy and tough. It touches them. It reaches their fragility and humanity.

Even across continents Sedlec continues to speak. Karel tells us of the time a film crew came with Jeremy Irons to film *Dungeons and Dragons*. 'They took the place over,' he recounts, 'and we think one of the film crew took one of the skulls because we got a letter from Customs saying someone in Hollywood was sending us a plaster skull. When it got here is wasn't plaster but real.' He believes they claimed it was plaster to get it through Customs without obstruction. 'We don't *know* that someone took it,' he concludes, 'but we know that someone returned it.'

'Do you believe the skull somehow communicated a wish to go back?' I ask.

'I don't believe in ghosts,' he replies with candour, 'but I think somehow maybe it did. That person could have disposed of it. Why did he go to the trouble of sending it back? It worked on his conscience.'

Karel tells us about the first time he touched one of the skulls in the ossuary after he had come back to take up his current position. 'I held it in my hands and I had a moment of real connection. I looked at it and thought – this was a person like me. It was very personal, like stroking my wife's head.' I notice his arms, the strength in his physical frame and immense energy in every gesture as he speaks. How it contrasts with this intimate tenderness.

When I question the claim that some of the bones are Polish, Belgian and Bavarian, he replies: 'We can't prove this, but it is legend. I am trying to figure out how this would be even possible.' He notes the difficulty of medieval travel. 'One legend has it they were moved here because it was said that you could be in heaven faster, that in three days in this soil your body would decompose. But of course we have found no chemical evidence for this.'

He is keen to sift fact from fiction in these legends. When I ask about the authenticity of Abbot Henry's visit to the Holy Land, Karel leaps to reach a large volume containing the latest articles and research on the ossuary. Brushing the sugar bowl out of the way with the back of his hand, he lays it out on the table between our coffee cups. In it are pages of charts, illustrations, architectural elevations, essays, all in Czech which I cannot read. Zuzana's head and his bend over pages that entice and elude me.

'Part of the story is true', Karel looks up in excitement, his finger poised on a page. 'The earth from Jerusalem is very likely. He did go there. Soil was often brought back from the Crusades. But he couldn't have spoken with the King of Jerusalem; there wasn't a king in Jerusalem then.'

Karel has been involved with this extraordinary place since his youth. It not only provides his employment, it also clearly engages his mental and emotional energies. He is as fascinated by its history as he is involved in the minutiae of its daily maintenance. So I am really surprised when he tells me he thinks it should be closed down. There is regret in his voice when he says this, but no hesitation.

'Why?' I ask, amazed.

His answer shows how much the place has become a part of him, how much that first intimate touch of skull has come to shape his imagination. 'Because they should be in peace. Two hundred thousand people come through here in a year. I apologize to the bones. I tell them I am sorry, but you are helping me to raise money for the cathedral.'

The bones are not artist's materials to him. They are not fragments, war trophies, victims or curiosities. Pierced, wired and glued in installations though they be, they are not the thing they have become, but the thing they were. They are people, neighbours, persons from the other side of midnight. I think I almost understand this. It is something similar to the way I am beginning to feel about the bones in my own charnel house at home.

* * *

Late in the evening, awash with coffee, stories and a wild array of skeletal images, Zuzana and I retired to our hotel aptly named 'The Executioner'. It was decorated, in black humour that I have been told is typically Czech, with baronial crests and suits of armour, limewashed walls the colour of raw flesh on which were mounted an axe, sword, spiky ball and chain and various unnamed instruments of torture. On one entire wall was painted, in medieval style, a festive betrothal or wedding feast at which a miscreant observer, tied to a post, is having his eyes plucked out by birds.

Beneath this, we perused a menu featuring dishes such as *katuv sleh* ('executioner's whip') and 'hangman's meat'. Curiously unattracted by these, we ordered the largest salad available, which arrived in a bowl for about six, and spent the next hour stolidly munching our way through slightly green tomatoes and clumsy hunks of cucumber while pondering our mortality, the sobriety of which was punctured at intervals by bursts of hearty singing from the large party room next door. Through the crack in the French doors, beneath a heavily framed picture of Holy Mary, came disorderly strains of '*Frère Jacques*' in stumbling rotation, which gave way to the local football song 'I'm from Kutna Hora'.

In the morning we negotiated our way towards payment through a minefield of exclamation marks which amused but failed to enhance translation. 'Receive Euro' a notice read, adding '(course according to daily offer of bank and exchange office!!!)', and 'Facilities for payment euro!!! And money-back only in Czech money!!!' Laughing with Zuzana, I unfolded a suitable number of Czech *koruna* from the correct bag of currency, hoping not to be left with too much over.

As I waited for these transactions to be completed, I was struck by the fact that currency is not the only thing here that keeps on changing hands and forms. The cathedral, once commandeered as a tobacco drying barn, now a world heritage site, has let its ossuary too be passed into other hands. It was this transfer of ownership that enabled the extravagant decorations we see today, since it was only when the monastery was abolished in the nineteenth century and its lands bought by the powerful Schwarzenberg family that Rint was employed as its new designer. The monumental bells might have been the work of a half-blind Cistercian, but Rint's were the garlands, the chalices, the skull-hugging cherubs, the monstrances, the columns and ropes of bones, the macabre chandelier. His is the signature of 1870 picked out in human finger bones.

The Schwarzenbergs left their mark too. This is for me perhaps the eeriest of all the decorations in the ossuary: the shield they commissioned that hangs across the screen of the bell in the northeast corner of the *kostnice*, a great coat of arms topped with a crown of skulls and bones. On the lower right quarter a bone raven, with a curved beak of human ribs, rises from the flat crest to pluck out the eye of a Turk. No actual Turk's skull was used, of course, but the message is clear – a Crusader's victory. This is not the only victory it seems to me that the coat of arms proclaims. Its very presence is a mark of ownership on the whole *kostnice*. In their family crest emblazoned in other men's bones, marks of pre-eminence and authority are chillingly declared. It is an image that lingered as we prepared to leave the city.

* * *

As we boarded the train to Prague the rain began. I hardly cared. We would be travelling for more than twelve hours – it was a good day for rain, a good day for staring out of windows and pondering, and I had so much to think about. I had expected the charnel houses would all be pretty similar, that they would all say more or less the same thing to me. What that thing was I didn't know, but I'd felt that seeing them I would begin to sense some kind of continuity. After all, they all shared a single common purpose – the dignified disposal of human remains. Hoping that visiting these other charnel houses would make me feel more at home with my own, I had come on this journey looking for resolution, peace perhaps. What I felt as the Czech Republic rolled by, blurred through rivulets of rain, was contradiction, irresolution and disharmony.

At the bone house in Czermna, there had been a clear sense of purpose. Once we had found the foreigners' cemetery the whole story began to make sense. The area had been fought over and ceded to one nation after another: Germans having been expelled after the Second World War and twenty-first-century Germans having paid for recent repairs, questions of belonging and reconciliation were clearly central to the project. One got the feeling that Vaclav Tomaszek had had an undivided purpose and that that purpose, however demanding, was knowable, achievable and achieved. The bones themselves were orderly; the quiet nuns with practised talks gave the skull chapel an air of regularity. In that place of strangeness and forgiveness, there was a simple story: a single founder with a deliberate design expressed in the restoration of order and dignity.

Sedlec gave me none of this. Instead there were impossible legends. An alchemical ossuary which changed its character in different periods. A legendary founder who may indeed have brought soil from the Holy Land, but certainly not after speaking to a non-existent king of Jerusalem. An ossuary, first monastic, then destroyed and rebuilt; open bones, over centuries scattered, gathered, piled up, wired, stolen, returned. Tales of Belgian bodies, Polish bodies, Bavarian bodies; people who put themselves and their families to no end of trouble, choosing Sedlec over any other place on earth, over the familiar and familial, because they craved that fabled three-day release of their souls to Paradise. Then there were the hated Hussites with cleavered heads – battle-weary skulls, that had been broken and grown over again, telling the fact if not the detail of raging brains exposed, agonies endured and partial healing. An unsettling cocktail of brutal fact and intriguing fancy, these wildly varied stories vied for my attention like unruly children.

Even in the arrangement of the bones themselves, at Sedlec I had sensed discontinuity. The solid mounded bells like hills, with remains grouped together in row upon row, made by their sheer numbers a statement of solidarity, a human foundation. The later garlands, the chalice, the chandelier, were things ephemeral in comparison; dangling in the arches the bones looked fragile, as if one malicious snip of wire could send them all clattering to the floor. Lenka, the souvenir-seller at the entrance, had reminded us when we entered that the decorations were not cosmetic or whimsical but Christian symbols and that the message of the installation was clear: *memento mori* – remember you are mortal. Do today the good you would see done. Seize the present which is real and fleeting. I could see the point of what she said. But the feeling of disquiet at the baroque installations was not appeased.

I don't know why. If it is acceptable to move, stack, arrange bones in a pyramid or in a colossal bell ('the voice of God'), why should it be strange to make them into garlands that represent the life and fecundity of God's world? Or into chalices brimful of wine – God's blood – or a monstrance, a display cabinet for bread – God's body – each in their way bearers of divine gift, marks of the goodness of the earth, fruitfulness of field and vineyard? I believed Rint had intended joy, but all I felt was a sense of the macabre.

Nowhere was this more strongly felt than when I looked at the Schwarzenberg family crest, for here were bones of all shapes and sizes sought not because they needed saving from the indignity of haphazard disposal, but chosen from among their fellows for the simple usefulness they provided to one household. Bones of all sizes seized from many bodies to create this manifesto of superiority. Bones that never belonged to any Schwarzenberg made to tell, in their death and forever, the superiority of the Schwarzenberg name, not only over them but also over Turks they had reputedly defeated and whose lands and farms and goods and chattels they had acquired.

Where the bells spoke to me of humility, the common humanity of us all, the Schwarzenberg crest spoke to me of pride, the singularity of the superior. Where the first left me feeling enlightened, at once standing on the edge of mystery and nearer to something true, the second left me feeling tricked by artifice, as if I had witnessed a theft that was unable to be rectified. The *kostnice* at Sedlec disturbed whatever peace I was trying to make with my own charnel house's bones.

I have seen how unresolved things can sometimes solve themselves if you just lay them aside for awhile. Along comes a conversation, a book, a dream; the conscious and the subconscious work together on the problem, conspiring in the corner of your busy days like crossword fanatics, and you find, when you go to look at the problem again, that it has changed. Its thorns have grown less prickly, it is a less puzzling colour. Sometimes it is no longer on the problem shelf at all but has grown wings of its own and flown (or feet perhaps and toddled off) – even the new shape of it you don't know, nor its mode of transport, if it has entirely disappeared.

This is what I did with Sedlec. For hours, against the window pane, elongated drops chased each other like small eels down rivulets of rain. My thoughts did much the same as I scratched busily in my lined notebook, registering my disquiet, examining as much of the roots of it as I could see, noting the images that came to mind, and then I left it. We were on the way to Prague again, and I had to clear enough space in my mind for whatever would befall us there.

I remember my first trip to Prague in 1990. A young American wife with her English husband, I went out of curiosity. We drove all the way from England in a red Peugeot 106, my adventurous parents in the back seat, slicing little circles of sausages for us at lunchtime and patiently folding and refolding maps.

It was a time of new beginnings: the end of European Communism and the reunification of Germany. We were all of us enthusiastic about what was happening in Central Europe and we drove through Berlin, where the jagged wall had just come down, celebrating liberty. At the spot where checkpoints had been we stopped, got out of the car, did a little freedom dance, took photographs, bought balloons from a trinket vendor. We were standing where people had done impossible things – dug tunnels underground, brazened it over high barbed wire, folded friends into the space in a car where a petrol tank should have been. They had risked everything for freedoms we considered commonplace.

Sometimes – fearfully, violently – they had lost these gambles. The weight of that fact saddened us and, suddenly feeling a little awkward in this strangely open unmarked space, we decided to let the balloons go. Together at first they bolted up then parted, each in turn riding its own current till they lost their tails and even their shape, drifting into specks of colour we could no longer follow with our eyes. One after another we lost sight of them all.

Back in the car, silent, we pressed on further into Eastern Germany and on towards Prague. Wonderful new things were happening; we hoped to glimpse the old before it disappeared. When I saw World War Two bullet holes in the sides of venerable Prague buildings I didn't think 'what a mess', but 'wow! what a great bit of history'. I wanted to go and put my fingers in the scars, see if deep down you could still sniff the whiff of gunpowder. Like Berlin, this was a city coming back to life. There was something vital in the air – like spring, like resurrection.

In those days historic guts of buildings were being devoured wholesale by the cranes and diggers of rejuvenation schemes.

McDonalds was rising, efficient and fatty, behind an eighteenth-century façade. It was stiflingly hot. There was no air-conditioning. We took a tram home every afternoon, filled the enormous bath in our hotel flat with cold water and took turns to lie in it like zooed seals.

When the sun went down we would emerge, explore the streets of the city centre, eating pizza in the Old Town Square, watching the astonishing astronomical clock as its skeleton Death rang out the hours. As night fell we let ourselves fall under the magic of Charles Bridge. Passing through its alternating pools of light and gloom, we searched among the bridge's thirty statues for St John Nepomuk and touched his shiny plaque, allegedly an assurance that we would one day return.

During all of my childhood in the United States, Prague had been, in my mind, primarily a satellite of communism. Associated with the enemy, it was a place that felt tinged with danger. Now I discovered that you really could walk halfway over the bridge and disappear in mist, just like in all the spy movies I had seen. That and the bullet holes meant that every stereotype was real after all, and as we drove west towards home, through forests of depressingly drab high-rise communist flats in decay, we hoped that the opening of the Czech Republic would bring something better for the people than more McDonalds.

Twenty years later I was on the train returning, more rather than less curious. It was not only post-Soviet changes that interested me now, and I had the advantage I had not had then of a companion translator. Returning through Prague station, Zuzana and I stopped at the Fantova Kavarna to savour the atmosphere and the coffee. There were six large brass-rimmed clocks mounted on the wall above six disused ticket kiosks. All of them stopped, all of them telling a different time. They seemed to me like the layers of

Czech history, coexisting and variant all at once. There were several Pragues here.

Where we sat, under the battered green dome, alongside the art deco phone booth, an old Prague remained remembered in the wall frieze that faced the entrance doors where giant bare-breasted ladies with strong stone socialist arms upheld the fluttering motto 'Prague, Mother of Cities'. Beneath all of this, as if arising literally from under the ground, another Prague of futuristic glass and gleaming steel was being constructed. And a bow-tie-wearing dynastic Schwarzenberg (His Serene Highness The Prince of Schwarzenberg, Count of Sulz, Princely Landgrave in Klettgau, and Duke of Krumlov) had lately become one of its senators.

As we waited for the Salzburg train that would take us, reluctantly, away from this station with its crumbling history above and its futuristic gleaming below, I thought of Sedlec with its unforgettable bones, put there not to be consigned to the past but in hope of the resurrection. Even those bleak bones are facing the future: a future not prophesied, as this station's was, by the clean lines of glass and steel – a future that can only be imagined, but in the hope of which all other futures shared.

I could end this chapter here, let the rebuilding of cities, of cultures, the restorations of cathedrals and charnel houses carry the weight of resurrection. But I know that the promise implicit at Sedlec was not primarily about that; it was about generations of ordinary people hoping to live again in some kind of resurrection body recognizably their own, and I cannot divert their quest entirely into metaphor. It would be a cop-out. Sedlec was started by a Cistercian drive towards simplicity that sought a better life, both here and hereafter, but what drove people to Sedlec in their thousands throughout the Middle Ages and beyond was a belief in a real and personal resurrection. What on earth were they thinking?

With that question in my head, and an awareness of my own resurrection ignorance, I started investigating and discovered that what they thought was not exactly what previous generations had thought about the resurrection. In fact, theories of the resurrection and images of the resurrection have altered much over time. When we speak of 'life after death' now, we usually mean the life that follows immediately after bodily death, but the earliest sense of 'resurrection' did not mean this. It meant 'new life after a period of being dead'. As the modern theologian N. T. Wright notes in his magisterial study on the resurrection, while pagans denied the possibility of resurrection, some Jews affirmed it as a long-term hope, and Christians claimed that it had already happened to Jesus and in the future would happen to them; but for all of them 'resurrection' was 'a two-step story'. It was in effect, life after 'life after death'. Wright notes that this meaning was constant throughout the ancient world until the second century.

In *The Resurrection of the Body* (Columbia University Press, 1995), Caroline Walker Bynum studies theories of the resurrection in Western Christianity from AD 200 to 1336. She notes that of all the 'so-called world religions' only those that arose in the Mediterranean Basin or the Middle East – Zoroastrianism, rabbinic Judaism, Christianity and Islam – hold a doctrine of the resurrection of the body. The Ancients, although they did write about life after death, never held that there would be a bodily resurrection. For Homer the body was real and the soul, after death, not more than a lamentable shadow of self, a wraith. For Plato or Cicero, the spirit was real and the body was a prison house. There might be life after death but not a resurrection; those who followed Homer knew they wouldn't get a body and those who followed Plato didn't want one. Resurrection was a radical and often offensive notion in the Greco-Roman world.

For those who believed it, it was also an imminently expected event. In the first millennium after Christ, Christians expected the physical return of Christ and the establishment of 'a new heaven and a new earth' right then and there. When this did not happen, new theories of the resurrection began to emerge, beginning with the 'seed'.

The oldest Christian metaphor for the resurrection of the body is the seed from I Corinthians 15, in which a grain of wheat falls into the ground and dies and lives again. The seed image is also present in Islam (Sura 56.60–1) and in rabbinic Judaism.

For early Christians the body remained an inescapable carrier of identity so that by around 200 AD both Tertullian, writing in Latin, and Irenaeus, writing in Greek, were defending the importance of the body as much as ever. But a paradox remained. As Walker Bynum notes: 'Body is flux and frustration, a locus of pain and process. If it becomes impassible and incorruptible, how is it still body? If it remains body, how is its resurrection either possible or desirable? To put it simply: if there is change, how can there be continuity and hence identity? If there is continuity, how will there be change and hence glory?'

Going back to the biblical image of the seed – if a sheaf of wheat sprouts from a seed buried in the earth, in what sense is that sheaf, which is new matter and a new structure, the redemption of the seed? How is the newly sprung wheat the same, and in any case why is similarity salvation? Early Christians such as Methodius, Basil, Gregory of Nyssa, the Syriac writers, Ambrose and Augustine all wrestled with these issues in the face of pagans who found the idea of resurrection perplexing.

The first-century pagan Celsus had claimed the body was worse than dung, and generations of writers added that it was a disgusting jar of urine, or a bag of shit, a prison of the soul, or an aching groan. The fourth-century theologian Gregory of Nyssa called the body a 'calamity' and wondered, unless it was freed from illness and brutishness, who would want it back again. Discussions such as this carried on through the third and fourth centuries and none of the great writers of the period solved the conundrum of retaining identity while allowing change.

Then in the 390s theologians came back to the first-century Church Father, Origen of Alexandria, who had noted that in fact continuity and transformation are already happening in the human body and that they happen all the time. 'For this reason, river is not a bad name for the body since, strictly speaking, the initial substratum in our bodies is perhaps not the same for even two days. Yet the real Paul or Peter, so to speak, is always the same.'

He wrote about this change that remains recognizable as being based on an *eidos*, or 'form' in the Platonic sense, a kind of plan coupled with a seminal capacity for growth and development. Origen's *eidos* is a pattern that organizes the flux but retains an essential propensity for growth. At once coherent and dynamic, it operates, as Walker Bynum notes, 'a bit like a genetic code'.

Although images of the resurrected body in Christianity continued to evolve over the centuries, what endured was the idea that the body was necessary to salvation because the body was necessary to any idea of self. By the time the Cistercians were moving across Europe towards Sedlec, the early image of seed that grows into a different and glorious sheaf was being replaced by the image of dust or 'earth', as the Cistercian Bernard of Clairvaux called it. His 'earthy' body represents both filth and decay and, at the same time, the stuff out of which the new, necessary and desirable resurrected body is made; to be 'earth' and 'dust' is to be the lowliness out of which something can be made.

His point is that resurrection is pure miracle, rather than a natural process. As Walker Bynum puts it, 'The idea of person, bequeathed by the Middle Ages to the modern world, was not a concept of soul escaping body ... it was a concept of self in which physicality was integrally bound to sensation, emotion, reasoning, identity – and therefore finally to whatever one means by salvation.'

So what were those people at Sedlec thinking when they gathered the bones into their charnel house? The remains at Sedlec were not regarded as mere biological waste; they were a necessary part of what it means to be a person – necessary even to the miracle of resurrection. For this resurrection was not going to be, argued Bernard, like the initial creation of matter, a creation *ex nihilo*, out of nothing, but a creation *ex vetere*, from the old, or even *ex terrae pulvere*, out of the dust of the ground.

As these ideas filtered down to less literate minds, common tradition had it that a femur and a skull were prerequisite for a resurrection, and to this day you will see many more femurs and skulls than anything else preserved in charnel houses and ossuaries. This is the ideological and intellectual framework in which the Cistercian charnel house at Sedlec was constructed and into which its thousands of bones were gathered.

Resurrection theories, of course, did not stop evolving in the Middle Ages. Seventeenth-century atomic theory suggested that all that was requisite for a resurrection was a single atom and, when eighteenth- and nineteenth-century New Testament scholars cast doubt on the historicity of miracles in general and in particular on the central Christian miracle, the Resurrection, believers began to conceive of the resurrection of Christ as an idea rather than a physical reality. Emphasis on the immortality of the soul increased and there developed a gradual preference for soul over body, so that many Christians, particularly in the rising Protestant tradition, conceived of life after death simply as a spiritual existence.

Even now, theories of the resurrection continue to emerge. Among the most recent are the ideas of the prize-winning quantum physicist John Polkinghorne; what intrigues me about these newest theories is that in a strange way they echo ideas that were present way, way back, in the days of Origen, before we imagined the resurrection in disembodied terms or conceived of the life beyond as angels with wings playing harps on clouds.

Polkinghorne notes, as have many before him, the continually changing nature of the human. 'What maintains continuity in the course of this state of atomic flux', he writes, 'is the almost infinitely complex information-bearing pattern in which the matter of the body is at any one moment organized. It is this pattern that is the human soul.' This pattern is not static, a given at birth, but may develop as character forms and experiences and decisions make us who we are. It is, he argues, 'a perfectly coherent possibility [...] to affirm the belief that the God who is everlastingly faithful will preserve the soul's pattern *post mortem*' so that it may be re-embodied again in a resurrection of the whole person.

At the crux of all these arguments lies a basic tension between continuity and transformation that I think is held in any concept of resurrection. What the ancient Church Fathers debated about bodies can be seen as well in the material rebirths of cities and nations. Wherever there is resurrection there is this tension between continuity and transformation – how much of the old is to be retained? What is essential in the old, and what is innovative about the new? How can these two be blended so that what emerges is recognizable but not a replica? Or how can the weaknesses of the old be transcended without destroying the essence of the thing?

As I discover new things about the development of beliefs

concerning the resurrection, the whole doctrine seems more and more significant to me because I see that, from earliest times, what was being debated was not only something supernatural but also something fundamentally human – this dynamic tension of continuity and transformation. Every day, in fact, we live this dynamic as our cells reproduce, making us always who we are and yet each day one day older either growing or ageing – in any case, transforming into what we will eventually be.

I can see now why it is that, over millennia and across cultures and despite our present-day mantra that only the empirically evident is real, we humans have not been able to lay down the idea of a life beyond this one, and we continue to wonder and debate what that life might imply. Questions about the resurrection are inescapable because they are really questions about what it means to be simultaneously and inextricably both spiritual and physical.

I begin to understand what Sedlec was telling me. Sedlec was about possibility and the quest to find a lasting hope. Its story is about resurrection, about what might be possible that we do not understand, about hoping in the midst of doubt, or the possibility that what we hope for may never be.

It is not so much about believing the impossible but believing that, because our knowledge is limited, there may be many possibilities of which we have not conceived. It is about leaving room for the improbable or at least the unproven; actually, not just leaving room, but actively making room. It is the daring act of staking a claim in the unprovable. That is what makes it hope rather than optimism, because it is active. It does more than wait to see what will be; it acts prior to proof. It is audacious.

The question that Sedlec wanted to ask me is simply this: Have you found a lasting hope? Despite the contradictions and discontinuities I found in Sedlec, the place has begun to make sense to me; its three-day resurrection myth is like a story that speaks of something bigger than itself. Thoreau, writing about a bean field, notes that the ear of wheat is in Latin *spica*, obsoletely *speca*, from *spe*, hope; and my mind jumps to Sedlec, because resurrection theories, starting from the grain of wheat onwards, are all about this one thing – a lasting hope.

Still I encounter a problem with the resurrection. For many people it is the mechanics of resurrection that seem incredible, but strangely enough it is not the question 'how' that most bothers me. The whole of human history is littered with things that were once deemed impossible. We know so much about matter and energy, but there is also much that we do not yet know and our knowledge is always changing. Five hundred years ago no one imagined light bulbs, or space travel, or genetic engineering. A decade or two ago saying we are made of stardust would have sounded like the stuff of a fairytale, and now it sounds like particle physics. So I do not find it hard to imagine the possibility of a bodily resurrection. Yet I do have a problem with the resurrection, and it is this: my belief in the possibility of resurrection does not remove the frustration of resurrection life seeming so far away. It is not so much the question 'how' as the question 'when'.

This is not helped by the fact that resurrection life is spoken of almost exclusively as if it were about what happens after you are dead – heaven, hell, maybe purgatory; torments and rewards. Such a resurrection is often painted by the most confident believers as a stunning future prospect that somehow renders present difficulties insignificant – in fact, so insignificant that those difficulties need not be addressed; wrongs need not be righted now since they will be righted forever in the sweet by and by.

Not only does this seem unreal to me, it also angers me that the idea of 'resurrection' which could be transforming should be used to placate. We hear that 'Life has conquered Death' and yet we all die; victory is claimed, though that victory is always, it seems, eventual. Sometimes I want to stand up and shout: 'Well if Jesus has won the victory why are we all in such a bloody mess?' And what good does believing in life after death do if it means you just put off living? If hope is hushed frustration, what good is it? And who would want such a hope?

The kind of resurrection that starts happening now in the ordinary present is the kind that most captures my imagination. Resurrection life in which somehow future joy breaks in on the present, as if time wraps around itself and what *will* be actually happens. I have sometimes seen bold changes in which people's lives are made new already, here, in this world, and the wonderful thing is that new life of that kind spills over. It spreads like watercolour soaking up across a glistening paper. This kind of resurrection hope makes me want to cheer.

I think about the many theories of resurrection just within Christianity and how, over thousands of years through images of seed and dust, the tension between continuity and transformation, those various resurrection theories are somehow never able entirely to leave behind the body. Many of us seem to have forgotten this, imagining, if we imagine it at all, life after death to be about a disembodied soul, a ghostly existence, something entirely spiritual. But my journey to Sedlec and the investigations to which it has led me remind me that whatever we mean by salvation is finally bound to a body.

This encourages me, for it helps me to see that my frustration with prevalent talk about the resurrection is not unfounded. Maybe it is right to be frustrated with an idea of resurrection that defers new life and takes it away from material reality. I have little idea what a resurrected body after death might be like, but I can have a very good idea of what a resurrected life might look like now. And that is something towards which one can turn.

To be hope at all (rather than some kind of vague optimism or fanciful dream) hope must have one foot in the mud. This is what I have come to understand. We think we need a dream. We are urged to 'climb every mountain' till we find it (roll Julie Andrews in slow motion on a mountain top). But what we really need is hope. Humans cannot live without it. We can do without many things: without holidays, without delicacies, without as much money as we thought we needed – even, as I have come lately to see, without the promise of a good prognosis. But we cannot live well for long without hope.

Hope is not the same thing as optimism. Optimism says that things will get better. Hope says that the good we envisage is the good we work towards. Optimism is largely passive: it is about waiting for what is better to come to you. Hope is active: it goes out and does. It falls and fails sometimes, but it is tenacious and unafraid, and it survives long after optimism is dashed. Optimism daydreams; hope has confidence. It is awake. It will not let go of the notion that the good is real, and that we can find it.

The three-day resurrection myth associated with the charnel house at Sedlec was what first invited me to discover more about the development of the doctrine of resurrection. The discontinuities there at Sedlec, between medieval mounds and Rint garlands, between the solemn and the frivolous, between the solidarity of anonymous skulls and the singular superiority of the Schwartzenburg crest, and the overarching question left unresolved – What are these bones, artist's material or sleeping people? – disquieted my thoughts. Now, they seem to me somehow fitting conundrums in a charnel house devoted so specifically to the doctrine of the resurrection – a doctrine which, from its earliest days of debate over continuity and transformation, has been both subversive of the prevailing culture and tangled in paradox.

4

Hallstatt

The early evening train we boarded from Salzburg towards Hallstatt was overcrowded. Lurching along its juddering corridors, we eventually found space in a carriage with three young women and a small, white, eleven-week-old chihuahua called Lila who opened up conversation in the way that babies can. Chatting until our fellow travellers departed, we reached Austria's lake region as true night was descending. Just before Steinkogler and Ebensee, Zuzana and I spied, through the darkening and reflecting glass, twinkling lights along a curve of shoreline, the bi-coloured opaque grey of night water and dramatic cliffs rising up out of it jutting into sky. Half-shrouded in mist, these rocky thrusts seemed somnambulant giants, or prehistoric behemoths.

As the train trundled on, my late-night mind wandered to a particular and powerful memory – another curious stone beneath the water that I encountered while snorkelling at Peanut Island off West Palm Beach in Florida. My husband and I, having left our girls with my sister on the beach, were stealing a very rare childfree moment, swimming along in masks and snorkels, learning a new way to communicate. Sign language had to do for everything: thumbs up, thumbs down, urgency indicted by a tapped shoulder, direction in the pointing of a finger, bubbles where words might have been.

It was not a silent world. There was, in my chest, a heart pounding fast with excitement that seemed to echo in my ears, and the steady rush of air down the long tube at the side of my head – in, out, in, out – loud as an engine. Purges too, like small volcanoes, expelling water, leaving in my mouth a faint taste of salt. Far from silent, there was such a roar of heart and lung down there that if we were going to make a success of communication we would have to listen with our eyes, attend to each other's every motion. I thought how romantic a thing this was to do on Valentine's Day – learn a new way of being alongside each other, a new intimacy – and I slipped my hand in his, in truth also a little frightened at the sharp-toothed barracudas and moray eels that swam with the bright Blue Tangs (dorsal fins like a short crew cut across the top of their heads) and tiger-striped Sergeant Majors in this strange new world.

Rounding a reef alongside a cluster of small yellow-tailed Schoolmasters, we signalled and then descended towards a large, smooth, brown rock that suddenly, within an arm's reach, shuddered, rolled on its side, folded itself in two and, with an enormous heave and shift, became an eight-foot manatee. A great, prehensile lip curled at the end of its stumpish snout, its small wide-set eyes opened in a circular fan, like camera lenses; registering the approach of a four-armed, four-legged, two-headed creature, the 'sea cow' swiftly turned away. Afraid of us as we were of it, it plashed its great flat paddle tail and disappeared into greater depths while we shot back, divided, our flippers pushing us independently to the surface at top speed.

Frightened and thrilled in equal measure, I rose to the surface, splashed hastily towards shore waving my arms at the children and shouting at the top of my lungs with utter joy, 'A manatee, a manatee!' Wading in further, clumsy in flippers, stumbling and raising my arms to heaven, I called, even though they had missed the moment, 'A manatee!' My eight-year-old daughter, wide-eyed and bewildered by my jubilant shouts, thought I must suddenly have been baptized with overwhelming love for all people. Why else would I be shouting with such joy, 'Humanity, humanity!'

That particular memory was triggered by the sight of a jutting rock, but how many memories are triggered by a smell, a taste. Sights, sounds, smells come to us and, completely unbidden, our senses immediately transport us to a memory, while at other times when we want to remember we simply cannot. We think we own memories, but maybe it is they who own us. We are shaped so much by them – by the ones of which we are conscious and perhaps even more by the ones of which we are not. Collective memories too, of our tribe and culture, have always shaped how we understand ourselves. It seems to me there is a tendency, in our day of globalization and modernization, to forget the local and historic, and I wonder whether we have counted the cost of our forgetting.

* * *

Having arrived in Hallstatt in deep darkness, we had seen nothing yet of the town. In the morning Zuzana called to me urgently to come and look. Wrapped in a cardigan, she had flung the French doors onto our balcony open to the most unexpected view; I stumbled out in haste, barefoot and clutching a shawl, to join her in shivering amazement. Not fifty feet from our balcony, a great wall of stone rose, through the dense mists, tall as the sky. This mountainside stretched eastward to the distant horizon, blocking from view anything but itself. Craggy and grey with shafts of gold running vertically through it here and there, its jagged face was flocked with clumps of spruce and cedar, and rippling white stripes which, when we looked hard, we could see were not lines at all but tumbling cataracts. There was so much personality in these

rock-faced mountains whose first harsh appearance was amelio-
rated not only by the interruptions of greenery, but also by this
restless presence of several kinds of water. The harder I looked the
more I could see that this apparently solid rock mass was, in fact,
permeated by water, that there was a particular ecology formed by
the contradiction of its solidity and the water's ceaseless flow.

Bewitched by this view, I could have stayed all day simply
watching the faces of this mountainside. White mists moved over
the patient rock face softly, like slow veils, by their movement, by
their thickening and thinning, alternately hiding and disclosing
deeply textured surfaces of green and grey. Protruding rocks became
a human face, an outline, a shadow, a rock again. Witches and old
men, hags and prophets rose and reclined in the play of sunlight on
the craggy stone. Pointed peaks of evergreens appeared and disappeared beneath her misty veils. Threads of water poured tirelessly
out of her sides, cascading white and fierce; everywhere there was
the sound of many waters. At her feet, where shrubs and grass met,
fast-flowing cataract-fed streams gushed down through the valley.
But what struck me most acutely, because I did not expect it at all,
was the mountain's effect, not on the surrounding earth but on the
sky. Her outline, the unmistakable, immovable vast shapes and
angles, brought the sky into relief, almost as if there wouldn't be
sky without them. The sky was all new, in this jagged interval, and
I understood with grateful clarity how often we miss what is always
with us.

As I reflect on that vision of sky from the distance of my writing
desk, I think that seeing things in relief is normally like this – a
kind of exercise in sideways vision. You look at something that has
previously appeared in one way and suddenly it is something else.
The same thing, only different. I think about the bones I have seen,
mountains of them, and how they bring the present day into relief.

It is as if our present wouldn't exist without them. Not only because of biology, the inheritance of DNA, not only because of invention – all the layers of things our ancestors have made that have brought us to modernity; it is not only because of what they have left behind, but because, if you learn to listen to the speech that is not words, they may speak still. Their dead yesterdays make present life leap with possibility, make the present moment alive and sweet. Then, on that Austrian balcony, it was only sky I thought of. How wonderful it was to truly see it.

In a maple close beside our balcony the song of a blue tit pierced that rock-angled sky like a needle. I could not stay shivering on the balcony. Breakfast beckoned and, in a dining room lined with skulls of mountain goats, antlers and horns of stags, a pleasant young woman in a dirndl served us creamy goat cheese and dark bread with eight kinds of jam, each more delicious than the last.

With a population of less than 1,000, Hallstatt is a small town and easily discovered. Our guesthouse was near the top of the Echterntal valley where 'Painters' Trail' leads away from town towards higher alpine meadows and the huge grey peaks of the Dachstein. Most of Hallstatt is crowded lower down along the lake edge. Exhilarated by the fresh air and the majesty of the mountains, Zuzana and I strolled in the direction of town past wooden cottages hugging the stream. Fitted with neat lean-tos and woodsheds, they were snug, mainly constructed in natural wood planks weathered dark brown, and painted here and there in white trim, or occasionally having windows picked out in green or blue. They looked natural there, as if they were made from the mountain's trees and had been accepted by her stones.

Everywhere there were signs that outdoor life was regularly let into these houses: antlers over the door, windowsill jars of cuttings, lace-trimmed white curtains blowing at the bottom of an open window. Red and pink geraniums would bloom in pots and flower-boxes in the summer. It looked like it would be perfectly idyllic in August, swimming and messing about in boats, wildflower fields in the foreground, mountains rising above. That day, however, the swollen stream was raging and fierce and I could not help imagining the distinct possibility of floods.

As we crossed the one-lane bridge, four children in flapping kagouls and wellingtons, happy on rickety bicycles, roared past us oblivious of the water beneath them churned to froth. In an instant I wished I lived here, that those children were our neighbours and my own girls riding alongside them. Nearer to town, Zuzana and I noticed a scar like a zip on the mountainside and two small cars running up and down its lines. We were almost at the salt mine and its funicular railway that would carry us to a vantage point at the entrance of the mine, more than halfway to the top of Salzberg, Hallstatt's main mountain.

* * *

Salt is the reason for Hallstatt. Its very name is derived from *hal*, the Celtic word for salt, and Old High German *stat*, settlement. Nestled in a scenery of high mountains, mirror lakes and bright white glaciers, rich in rare flora and fauna, serviced by well-marked hiking trails and mountaineering cabins, swimming sites and sailboats, it would be easy to imagine that Hallstatt is primarily a place of leisure. It is in fact the oldest known industrial community in the world. Salt extraction began here in the Middle Bronze Age (late second millenium BC) and formed the basis of the area's prosperity up until the mid-twentieth century.

The town is bordered to the south by the glacier-glazed Dachstein, at 2,996 metres the region's highest mountain, and in the west by the Gosau ridge and the Gosau lakes. At its eastern edge runs Hallstattersee, a lake so clear it mirrors with marvellous precision the mountains that rise along its side. The visual impact of the whole Dachstein-Hallstatt region is dramatic, huge mountains rising abruptly from narrow valleys, but nowhere is this more magical than when the mountains come, fjordlike, straight to the water's edge.

At eight and a half square kilometres of lake, Hallstattersee is about half the size of England's Windermere, though it has very nearly twice its depth. Squeezed between rock and water, land is precious here; every square metre is utilized and, as the medieval town grew, Hallstatters began building also on the *mühlbach*, an artificial promontory out into the lake formed from the mining debris dumped over centuries. Much of the present-day town is clustered here. Gathered round a small triangular market square, the stone and timber Hallstatt houses lean in close proximity, tall and narrow, making maximum use of the restricted space and the steep topography. Little alleyways run between the rows of houses, up stone steps and sometimes over arched bridges where one of the several streams makes its way to the lake. Small boats are tied to the side of streamside houses whose walls are washed by the ceaseless flow of water.

Part of Hallstatt's charm, it seemed to me as I walked its narrow streets, was the unspoilt aesthetic of these historic buildings. Much of the town looked as if the nineteenth and twentieth centuries had somehow never arrived. It felt as if it were a place set apart, and for much of its life it has in fact been largely inaccessible. Until the late nineteenth century there were no roads into Hallstatt. You either came by boat or on foot. The earliest salt miners and merchants had carried their wares by water. In such a remote place visitors are rare. There are no strangers. Everyone is known and everything remembered. It would seem natural that people living so remotely and intimately might develop a particularly intimate and idiosyncratic way of commemorating their dead. What I find more intriguing is the timing of Hallstatt's peculiar charnel house tradition, for it was only a generation or two before the first road ended their deep isolation that their tradition started. As the eighteenth century turned towards the nineteenth, and the nineteenth ushered in unparalleled changes, it was as if the people of Hallstatt were turning remembering into an art. They were not the only village to paint the skulls of their dead. Other Alpine and Bavarian villages did the same, but only Hallstatt kept the tradition going. This is the art I have come to witness – not only the art of painting that they developed, but the art of remembering.

Meanwhile, in the world outside Hallstatt, technological and mechanical progress was levelling mountains and bridging gulfs to usher in a new industrial age. Progress, not recollection, was the urge. Engineering was an heroic endeavour; inventors were gods, and God was seen by Deists as a kind of inventor, the great 'mind' manifest in the laws of nature. Gravity, friction, energy, force – to discover ways of understanding and harnessing these was to become almost a god oneself.

In America, the Pacific Union and Grand Union railways, in one mighty simultaneous effort, pushed towards each other with bright thrusts of steel to build one great chain linking east and west. Opened on 10 May 1869, it had taken only three years for the lines to join, and suddenly the unthinkable was real – in eight days and at the cost of $65 (economy) one could traverse a continent.

In Paris Gustave Eiffel erected *La dame de fer*, his iron lady, in just two years. Completed in 1889, in time for the World Fair, it was abhorred by many who found it to be a blot on the Parisian cityscape. Novelists Alexander Dumas and Guy de Maupassant were among the cultured of the day who are thought to have hated it. By others it was equally and oppositely admired. The Wild West pistol-toting showman Buffalo Bill with his crew of Indians wowed the crowds there on his European tour; when the inventive businessman Thomas Edison came to visit the tower he entered in the guest book on 10 September 1889:

> To M Eiffel the Engineer the brave builder of so gigantic and original a specimen of modern Engineering from one who has the greatest respect and admiration for all Engineers including the Great Engineer the *Bon Dieu*, Thomas Edison.

He left us with the phonograph, the moving picture camera, the lightbulb, the international manufacturing enterprise General Electric and the motto: 'Genius is one percent inspiration, ninety-nine percent perspiration.'

Edison's motto somehow gives voice to a larger determination to be the determinators, the ones in charge, the ones taking Fate by the balls and shaking it upside down. In European cities large and small this progressive urge meant roads and drainage, sewers and tunnels, whose construction often entailed, as it had done in Paris and Sedlec, the removal of cemeteries and the exhumation of remains that added thousands of bones to many of Europe's charnel houses. The exhumed bones were often tumbled like rubble into overflowing charnels; these were not people but waste that needed particular handling, much in the way we might handle toxic waste today. The past was an encumbrance, and it was the duty of forward-thinking persons to eradicate those things that impeded progress.

Physical and philosophical change on a scale of such magnitude would eventually reach and alter even the rippling shores of Hallstattersee and the remote market town of Hallstatt. Although it had been settled, industrial and internationally commercial for several millennia, not a single road came and went from Hallstatt.

Then, in 1890, a year after the Eiffel Tower, the first road into
Hallstatt appeared – one that today still hugs its western edge, made
in part by the blasting of antediluvian adamantine rock. Once you
got to Hallstatt, access within the town itself was no easier. Access
between houses on the river bank was by boat or over the curious
'upper path', a small corridor that passed through adjacent attics
(part of this route still remains).

Roads brought visitors as well as traders. Once nineteenth-
century writers, poets, painters discovered Hallstatt and the
Dachstein, the place became a desirable destination, not because
of its salt, but because of its flavour – that peculiar blend of rugged
nature and nestled charm. Most of the leading painters of the
Biedermeier school found inspiration here. In fact, theirs was the
'painters' path' that had departed from near our guesthouse. The
path Zuzana and I took that morning down from the valley, they
took up, away from the lake and its hill-hugging houses, up to the
higher pastures and the ragged peaks beyond.

The aristocracy of the Hapsburg Empire who spent the summer
in the Salzkammergut had already discovered the region; Emperor
Franz Josef had built his summer villa in nearby Bad Ischl. But
Hallstatt had remained remote. In the wake of poets and painters
came tourists, and hotels, and ferry links to the railway. From
earliest times traders had come to Hallstatt to buy the mountain's
salt; what the tourists wanted to take away with them was memories.
Hallstatt's main commodity was changing.

Aboard the clackety mountainside funicular, the first view we
gained of Hallstatt town was not the serene watery view most
tourists have as they arrive by boat, but a screechy, bird's-eye sky
view, looking down from high above. Noisily gobbling track, the
funicular climbed up while we looked vertiginously down, gaining
above the clatter of the track an immediate sense of the crowded

nature of the town, its complete dependence on an awkward and magnificent topography that has compressed its streets and cropped its growth.

All its life Hallstatt had been clipped, like a bonsai tree, at the root. Riding 850 metres up the funicular it got smaller, and smaller still, as we ascended. I was only a third of the way up the first mountain and already it wasn't just the smallness of Hallstatt with its toy cars and its tiny roofs that I was looking at, but the size of all humanity. This is what the Alps can do for you, make you look at yourself in a different scale: diminutive humanity. How we love and hate to see this. Courageous, tenacious humanity – how long we have been living in this rich, wild and impossible place. But I didn't know that yet. As I climbed with Zuzana on the short funicular jaunt I only knew that we were going halfway up the mountain and walking down the other side to the charnel house. What we discovered on the way was another person's bone discovery.

Johann Georg Ramsauer, discoverer, was a native of this place and for most of his life he didn't know about it either. Born in Hallstatt in the icy spring of 1795, he grew up by the shores of its lake, in the lee of its magnificent mountains, clinging, like every other Hallstatter, to the hospitable side of this glacial rock. He was apprenticed to the mine and worked his way to the top, becoming mine operator, and living in the Bergmeister's house – the Rudolfsturm – that sits like a tower at the plateau of Hallstatt's upper valley. By the time he was king of the castle, the Rudolfsturm had outlived its usefulness as a defence against invaders and been turned into a large family house. Here, in this white stucco medieval fortress-turned-homestead, Ramsauer raised twenty-two children.

Then, in 1846, when he was 51 and had already fathered more children than most men dream of, he made a discovery that would revolutionize the archaeological world. It is said that Vaclav Tomaszek discovered the bones in Czermna when he was out walking with his dogs. Johann Ramsauer was just going about his business at the mine when he stumbled upon the graves that turned out to be the Hallstatt necropolis – approaching one thousand Bronze Age burials with very well-preserved remains and artefacts including tools, vessels and ornaments.

His timing was serendipitous, for this was the era of the artefact. The same improvements that had joined the east and west coasts of America had also opened foreign lands to travellers as never before. From Jerusalem and Sinai, from Damascus and Cairo, curios and artefacts and even mummies had become the coveted badge of the cultured élite. In 1833, one inveterate traveller reportedly observed to Muhammad Ali, the ruler of Egypt, with a certain panache, that 'it would hardly be respectable, on one's return from Egypt, to present oneself in Europe without a mummy in one hand and a crocodile in the other'.

In such an age of curios and artefacts, it would have been unusual if, when the imperial court visited Bad Ischl for a season, some members of the court had not paid a visit to Ramsauer's site. In fact Emperor Franz Joseph did visit several times. When his party happened to be present at some new uncovering, they did not feel it importunate to request a souvenir, and Ramsauer found himself unable to refuse. In this way many valuable pieces were lost; nevertheless, Ramsauer was not a complete blunderer. He recorded the finds in his notes and in some cases had replicas made. In the absence of modern-day photography, he enlisted a local artist to paint the findings *in situ*.

Isidor Engl's paintings can still be seen at the Museum of Natural History in Vienna. There is great precision in them; they are mainly graves. Many graves, in gold, sepia and grey, with colour translucent as dragonfly wings, executed with a lightness I did not expect. Oblong graves like eggs, with the lids lifted off, revealing folded bones like flightless chicks. I had not thought to find them beautiful, but there is such life in their postures that I am taken by surprise. They are not laid like solemn soldiers in reposeful rows, but each placed in a position in which you might expect to find a person in life, as if whoever laid them there did so with a personality in mind. This person had attitude, says the skeleton with arms akimbo; this person danced. There are hallelujah hands raised in jubilant expectation, femurs crossed at the knees like a large X, or one straight, one raised, as if frozen in the move of a necroplastic jive. There are arms wrapped (protectively or lovingly) around containers. One has his arm positioned so that his hand is just where a scabbard might have hung and his knees are slightly bent, ready to spring. One is positioned arms raised, knees bent, torso twisted, literally kicking his heels with glee. Four are buried in pairs, one with an arm around the other. Many of them lie with possessions such as tools, bowls, vessels, jewellery, basins near their heads as if there might have been water or food ready for them when they woke up. Two of them are children.

It must have been amazing to discover these people, each so different from the last; to wonder what the next grave shell would reveal. Wherever they believed they were going, it looks to me as if they thought it was going to be good. And as if they expected to be themselves there. The evidence suggests they intended not only to live again, but to need the things we need: food, tools, laughter, common sense, quick-wittedness, love. Each of these intricate and fascinating watercolour graves is a capsule of life.

What archaeologists learned from Ramsauer's discovery was that Bronze Age and Early Iron Age Europeans were much more sophisticated than had been appreciated. The extent and technique of the mining shows it to be no amateur effort but a highly organized and managed production-driven enterprise, dependent not on passing trade but sustained by systematic transport and delivery. There was evidence of trade as far afield as Greece, and imported luxuries that included amber, ivory and glass. Ramsauer's discovery led to a redefinition of the periods of European history, so that the predominant Central European culture from the eighth to the sixth centuries BC became known as 'Hallstatt Culture'.

I wonder if Ramsauer knew how much work he was committing himself to when he set out on this task. I wonder whether his twenty-two children saw much of him. During his time as director of the excavations from 1846–63, he eventually unearthed nearly a thousand burials. It took him 18 years. It changed both the method and the measurements of archaeology forever.

* * *

The antiquity of the salt mines made me feel tiny; the mountain made me feel this too. Where the bird's-eye view ride on the funicular emphasized the smallness of our physical size, the archaeology at the top reminded Zuzana and me of both our recent arrival in the history of humankind and the extreme brevity of our stay. Not only were we small, we were also temporary. Upstart ants, if you like.

Over millions of years carbon-dioxide-enriched water seeped through this soil, travelling down into the ground. Dissolving the rock, the water created sink-holes (dolines) and extensive caves that served a whole subterranean drainage system. That was what I had seen that morning from my hotel balcony, as if the mountain were weeping, or bleeding water. The very salt here is the remainder of trapped seas. A sea trail is left, too, by the fossil-rich formations that abound in this region. Early salt miners of Hallstatt collected ammonites and sold them along the way as they travelled the rivers delivering their salt. A nineteenth-century German naturalist identified bivalves, nautiloids and ammonites in red limestone clusters, all in the region of the mine. Conical-shelled orthoceratids too had swum there, with eyes like the heads of screws, their long food-seeking tentacles sweeping out over trumpet mouths. Fossil selling has been going on for thousands of years. Local venues still sell them today.

We call Earth the water planet, swirling blue and white when viewed from the moon. Solid as we feel it to be, we know that it is more sea than mountain, more water than earth. But it is also a salty planet. At our current rate of extraction it would take about 250 million years to extract as much salt as there is in the oceans of the world. If we could extract all the salt of the sea at once and distribute it over the landmass, the world would be covered in a salt layer one hundred metres high. In Hallstatt, the salt of ancient trapped seas is extracted by turning them to seas again and pumping out brine as dense with salt as the Dead Sea. A brine pipeline, built of 13,000 tree trunks (spruce and fir) hollowed out and fitted together, was started in 1597, and took a decade to complete. A modern pipeline still transports brine to the salt works at Ebensee and Traunsee, and now a footpath, the Brine Trail, runs above the pipes, dropping from the Rudolfsturm all the way past Hallstatt to neighbouring towns and villages. Along its way you can still spy former entrances to the mines.

* * *

Behind the Rudolfsturm tower Zuzana and I began our descent on the pipeline trail marked out with steep steps and rustic railings through a wood of buttercups, mossy trees and dappled light. Lush ferns and underbrush covered the forest floor. Swift-flowing streamlets poured over limestone, in and out of small pools, tumbling wildly between jutting rocks and mossy hillocks sprung with late primroses and dark purple ajuga. This was fairyland and I wished my daughters were here to love it with me. Conforming to the demands of steep descent, the path switched back and turned, rose over a racing stream on little wooden bridges and twisted around an outcrop of stone. Perpendicular and lean, long firs and sycamores stretched skyward yearning for light. Under their tall trunks the canopy was high. Where sunlight dappled this woodland the moss brightened to an eye-catching vivid green, then shaded into loden again. Along the path *Dryopteris filix-mas*, the common dark green male fern, unfurled in friendly clumps. Nestled at the rock's base smooth spears of hart's tongue, *Asplenium scolopendrium,* glistened with droplets the stone had wept. The path narrowed and grew steeper as we descended towards the Millbrook and we noticed that the stream was picking up volume and speed.

The headstreams that feed into this torrent, and swell terribly as the winter snow thaws, once devastated Hallstatt in the floods of 1884. Such a terrifying force of unleashed water was not hard to imagine since it was raging all around us at the Millbrook waterfall, dampening the path and making our going slippery. Parting mist revealed an island of rock in the frothy stream below, craggy and bare except for one tenacious cedar whose roots had managed to cleave a foothold in the bald rock surface. I was amazed at its survival and at the branches and trees on either side of the cascade's cut that, half-torn from their bearings by floods, had refused to die but grown up towards light from sideways, branches rising like Arabic script from a horizontal baseline.

So deafening was the stream's spring roar that, as we approached the Millbrook, speaking became difficult. Resorting to sign language and the guide ropes along the trail, we dropped along the path through 'Hell's Hole', a wild, romantic crevice in the stone with precipitous drops above and below. Here where the trail was at its steepest and the rock faces became more pronounced, modern defences of cable, nets and posts anticipated an avalanche of stone. The path was wet from mist, and water dripped from the cliff edge above almost as steady as rain, from which an inadequate umbrella failed to protect us. We had come in foolish street shoes, and the wild beauty of the place unfooted me further. I felt as if my feet and my mind were sliding both, losing their bearings somewhat in the roar and blur of constantly moving water thrashed upon immoveable stone – a drunken marriage of motion and station, a clash of the permanent and the transitory, time immemorial and time fleeting. My hands felt along the stone outcrops for handholds, my feet losing traction slightly on the gravelly path, and I skidded to a halt.

We paused to view the torrent, the trees, to smell the sweet, wet, sharp green thrusts of spring. Around me all was a paradox – rush and stability, deafening sound crashing against the implacable silence of mountain. Like a fern or a sapling cedar, I too clung to this rock face, caught between a need for light and a thrilling wish to stay forever here in a rupture of stone and water, verdant and secret. This life was lush and grasping, akin to the untamed and untameable. There was nothing whimsical here. There was no mercy in the water; it was nature we smelt in the wet mist, wild as a tiger. We shivered. Our spring coats were not sewn for this.

On the other side of '*Durch Die Hölle*', looking back up towards the waterfall, I could see from below that the cedar tree island was not an island fist at all but a tall column some fifteen metres high, only the top of which could be seen from above. Speechless, I pointed at this revelation; it was not just the sound of raging water that rendered me silent. I wondered how many hundred years it had stood like that, alone in the tumbling stream, and how many more it would be before it was completely worn away. Before its roots perished and it was sucked in one greedy gulp down the wet throat of torrent.

Beneath the rock that overhung the footpath fat droplets fell. Round, and lit up with light refracted through departing mists, they were like small fat lightbulbs that, coming from such a height, seemed to fall in slow motion. Then with last-minute haste they hurled themselves on the stony path and smashed, bouncing up into liquid fireworks. Delighted by this spectacle, we at last abandoned our attempts at inadequate sheltering and, in silent agreement, put our faces directly in the line of fire, letting them be drenched, opening our mouths, dodging to catch the bright wet lights as children do snowflakes. Lips, eyelids, throats damp with pinging drops that pricked like stings, we found ourselves, hands outstretched, palms upwards, unbounded, laughing with the abandon of children or lovers.

Two middle-aged couples coming up the path in hiking boots and weatherproof coats and carrying walking sticks like ski poles stared at us curiously, smelling something strange in us – joy or freedom – or maybe the look was one of mere incredulity that we were there, in city clothes, Zuzana with a half-collapsed umbrella, me clutching a damp notebook. For my own part I thought it was they who, despite the correct attire, could never belong in this wildness. They had no eye for a tiger and looked as if the only thought on their minds was which cake they should have for tea.

Subdued by this intrusion, we continued our descent, the path becoming markedly less steep as we passed disused mine shafts, and decked and balustraded viewpoints where tourists might stop to admire the lake below where sleek sailboats sliced the slate-blue water. We did not stay. Around us there was too much fiddling with lenses and the strain of retained smiles.

The path eased still more, grew tamer and tamer till all that was left of the wildness was the meekest kind of wild I know: wildflowers, bright and merry, tiny and brave, poking their proud heads through moss and grasses to view the world with curious eyes. Some I knew by name: buttercups, thistle, cornflower greeted me like old friends, strangely out of place in this scene that had been so far that day filled with many and various kinds of newness.

I spied a patch of something yellow with which I was not familiar in England but which in America we call vetch, and this seemed stranger still, as if it had leapt continents and oceans to find me here. Beside a stone, the cousin of an aquilegia I know had sprouted, its leaves simpler than the garden one, with less dense foliage, the stem more apparent and fragile and flowers the deep, dark colour of a copper beech. On either side of the path at irregular intervals cow parsley punctuated the green undergrowth like sprigs of lace, and once a wild clematis wound its skinny way along a hawthorn twig. Around a bend in the path I was surprised and delighted by a bright wild rose just coming into bud.

The path switched back now, zigged and zagged, and was well worn. Something suburban rose up from the hillside to meet us. It was a small pavilion perfect in that now light-falling rain for a picnic lunch, which we unpacked and ate under a roof and pillars roughly carved with scratched records of illicit couplings and teenage love. I chewed old bread, watched a small bird flitting in the branches close beside me, and found I had no appetite for the last remaining piece of fruit. There was nothing here I wanted to see: not the names of who loved whom, sad in their historic inaccuracy, inscribed with a forever that I fear has failed; not the educational notices that told the names of wildlife I could hope to spy; not the steel poles set in concrete that formed a handrail to what had become a municipal path.

We would soon approach the town and find at last the crypt we had come so far to see, but all I wanted to do right then was climb back up to the waterfall and beyond. My head was full of sounds: the thrilling roar of water, the beautiful seduction of stinging drops – I wanted no more language in translation. Bursting with undigested life, a little drunk with wild beauty, a town and its pedestrian pathways seemed profane to me. So close to my destination, I wanted to flee. I was not afraid of death, the skulls, or the crypt; but afraid that I would lose the direct flow of life I had felt coursing through my veins on that waterfall walk. It wasn't the skulls that could take this from me. It was the living, with their polite notices and explanatory leaflets, with their civility and customs, their neat hedges and shops full of postcards. So close to my destination, I wanted to turn and run up the mountain passes till I found a shepherd's hut in which to make a quiet nest and spend a thousand days in craggy thoughtfulness.

We had an appointment, however, and a destination to reach. It was specific, it was small, and it was waiting. I sighed. Packing up the last remaining remnants of lunch, we left the love-scratched pavilion and took the well-worn trail down into town. The scene grew increasingly tame. Here and there the path had been filled with concrete. Lily of the valley that had strayed up the hill from town gardens rose incongruously between the damp fern and woodland scrub. We were at the very edge of town in steep descent looking down from above. Voyeurs that we were, we peered into the tiny courtyards that passed for gardens, spied a peek of green grass, a slice of picnic table, a plastic climbing frame, hints of the kinds of lives that hummed below oblivious of our prying eyes.

Then, suddenly, the multi-tiered spire of St Mary's church came into view, slate roof over white painted stone. One more twist of path landed us at the outer edge of a small terraced churchyard, well-kept and tiny, with small rectangular graves over each of which stood wooden markers bearing names, crucifixes, dates, protected from the damaging effects of weather by neat little peaked roofs. On one side, the mountain we had just descended rose abruptly; to the other side of the stone terrace a wrought-iron railing protected us from a sharp drop to rooftops below and there was, as the sun emerged from cloud, a shimmering view across the lake. Such water and sky and sunlight – I turned my face to praise them all.

Well below, we saw among the crowded rooftops the spire of a Protestant chapel, plain as this one was highly decorated. It was the feast of Corpus Christi, the Body of Christ – that feast day in which Christians celebrate Christ's instruction to his followers to remember his body and his blood in the Eucharist, or Mass – and Hallstatt was full of merrymakers in dirndls and lederhosen bearing boughs and blossom and laughing after beers. That morning the lake had been peppered with them, standing in boats like gondoliers, or perched on boat's benches, decked in festive best, bringing in the boughs.

Ducking beneath arches of twisted blossom, we entered the church where the boughs had been bundled together to look like young trees. There were candles and a gilded reredos, and every-where the damp smell of spring. Next to the church there was a small cottage and at its door the man I thought we had come to meet. Zuzana and I turned to see him smiling in our direction a little merrily, a little indulgently, as if he were pleased to see us and knew perfectly well who we were even before we had recognized him. I liked his gentle smile. And his boiled wool Austrian coat with intricate horn buttons, and his smooth white hair.

* * *

August Stögner is the last skull-painter of Hallstatt. He was once her priest and in his retirement has taken up painting – landscapes mostly, which tourists buy in the summer. He wanted to know whether we would like to see his studio. It was right there in the little cottage that, he told us, was once the gravedigger's house. Up two steps and through a door over which hung the lintel marked 1802 we entered the first of two rooms, a hall really, against the walls of which were propped a crop of paintings ready for framing.

The studio was light and homely. A tiled coal-fired heater chased the spring damp; pots of paint and dirty paintbrushes populated every surface. Canvases empty, started, and nearly finished stood on easels and lay on tabletops. The walls were hung with modern renditions of the Dachstein and Hallstattersee in strong hues with bold outlines. Not Biedermeier exactly, but pieces that would be easy to hang in almost any house in Western Christendom. I bet he sold plenty. This studio was where he worked; it was also where he painted the skulls.

It is no longer common practice for Hallstatters to be moved into the ossuary when they die, though there is the odd inhabitant alive who still wants this service and August has promised to accommodate them when their day comes. We stepped outside.

'First they are buried', August said, pointing to the small neat churchyard with its well-tended graves. 'Catholics here, on the first terrace; Protestants there, in the lower terrace.' I had seen the plain spire of the Protestant church in the town below. Perched on the promontory next to the lake, they have no ground for the dead.

'They stay for only about ten or fifteen years.' He waved his hand in the direction of the graves casually, as if they were feckless neighbours. 'It depends how soon we need the places, but after they have had enough time the bones are removed.'

I glanced at the graves with their simple wooden crosses and wondered whether they knew, these brave mountain-hugging people, whose places they would take.

'The skulls are yellow when they first come out, and we put them there.' He pointed to a small shelf under the eaves of the gravedigger's house. 'It is in the open air, but up out of reach of animals and protected from weather. There they bleach.'

'Ah, by sunlight', I said.

'And by moonlight', he added with a mischievous twinkle, as if a skull by moonlight were a playful thing to see.

There was something not only jocular in his manner; the way August said it made bleaching seem an important and necessary step. I wondered why that was, and what was the significance of this bleaching. Was it purely aesthetic, creating a blank page, a better surface for painting? Or was there some kind of piety at play, some sense of ritual cleansing prerequisite to being reunited with one's family and friends? It seemed to me a final humility was conferred during that time on the shelf. Whatever one has been in a lifetime, there one is no longer the determinator of anything. One no longer grabs life and shakes it upside down. In full public view and in all weathers, naked, one simply waits.

I knew that frost and sunlight were the old-fashioned natural bleaches of the Victorian laundress, but I had never imagined the moonlight bleaching of a skull. Still, as sunlight rippled over the surface of the deep lake below, it was easy to imagine the bright illumination of a full moon, and a patient skull unblinking, waiting and whitening in eyeless silence. It was easy to imagine how the bleaching skulls presided over babies and children, cheesemongers, miners, lovers and rogues passing through the churchyard on their diurnal and nocturnal assignations. Did any of the living nod, I wondered, did any cower or shift, just a little uneasily, under their boiled wool coats?

The families choose, if the dead have not previously done so, what kind of decoration the skull painter paints. Most families choose a simple crown from a range of four traditional designs: ivy, laurel, oak and rose. Ivy for faithfulness, laurel for victory, oak for glory, and rose for love. Apart from two small skulls with snakes where garlands should have been, painted bitterly in 1820 when the gravedigger's two children died, the designs are not usually idiosyncratic or individualistic, although in recent years some have made exceptional choices – to be commemorated as a miner, for instance. The choice of decoration does say something about the person, but perhaps most importantly the painted skull says that they belong to this community and its culture.

Gradually the ossuary tradition is being replaced with cremation. At the feast of All Souls, Hallstatters come in strength to pay their respects to their kind and kin, but most days there are more tourists here than villagers. August thinks he will be the last skull-painter of Hallstatt. He understands the aversion to being an object of interest to tourists – being photographed and posted on some stranger's blog or Facebook page as a quirky holiday snap. But he seems a little sad at this unique and tender history ending. These are people he has known and loved, baptized, married, counselled and cajoled.

Present-day Hallstatters are not used to seeing skulls on the bleaching shelf any more. I wonder what they will make of the last one when it appears. I wonder whether they will feel awe or revulsion, interest or fear. I wonder whether they will respect the unprotected dead or whether some raucous youth will come along one night on a dare and contemptuously knock it off its ledge. I wonder what promises will be made beneath it in the middle of the night. When the last skull is bleached white as moonlight, August will take it down from its fox-proof ledge. In his studio, the skull cradled in his hand, he will lift the brush.

* * *

Carved out of the limestone cliff face, Hallstatt ossuary is entered by a wooden door, which when open is the only source of natural light. August paused with his hand upon the door handle. It was not a place for stories or for speaking. He would leave us to our thoughts and wait outside. I was grateful for this unexpected reprieve from explanations. Grateful too to find that, although a few leaflets were available, there were no tour guides with microphones within, no busloads of tourists without, no femur-brandishing nuns.

The cave is roughly hewn. So small a tall man might stoop to enter, it can be crossed in three strong paces, its breadth in no more than four or five. Plain whitewashed walls rise from floor to ceiling and back to floor again in one simple spanning arch so that it is shaped like an almond, like an eye that is closed, its light-admitting door the pupil; along its far wall a sheet of polished metal mounted to reflect candlelight, like its retina.

A closed eye sharpens memory. I often close mine to remember, or to write. Sometimes, when I have misplaced my fingers on the keys, I open them to find a whole page of typed goobledygook that I have to retrieve from memory. Despite this annoyance there are times, when I am working hard to dig from the corners of my brain a perfect word, when only closed eyes will do. And so I instinctively understand this closed eye as a repository of the village's memory, and I feel particularly privileged to have been admitted by a momentary blink.

Straight ahead, raised a little above the skulls, there stands a crucifix. The smoke from votive candles, invisible to me, has by its constant presence coloured the ceiling above this bleeding Christ the light grey of a pigeon's breast. All around, on three sides of the cave, simple wooden shelves at hip height remind me of the large tabletops in my grandmother's cellar used for wintering apples. These shelves, however, house ranks of skulls twelve or thirteen deep, the space beneath them packed tight with femurs. With empty sockets and vacant noses, and with missing teeth, these skulls are like those we have seen everywhere; and yet they are not like any other skulls we have seen at all. Roses, ivy, oak and laurel, all of which I have seen this morning on my walk on the Pipeline Trail, I meet here again: cuttings of all that wildness transposed here onto these dead bones. It is the queerest sight – these skulls, universal emblem of death, overlaid with flowering fecundity.

Zuzana and I point and whisper, noticing the shapes and colours, and the tidy arrangement of families. How soft the roses seem, how proudly each green wreath crowns its skull an emperor. Across the forehead in blue or black is painted in beautiful old gothic script, beneath the dates of life and death, the person's name.

It is impossible not to feel that these are people. Sedlec's anonymous mounds and commandeered mandibles are as distant from this arrangement as are Czermna's gathered remnants; these skulls have been treated with the loving attention that you would give to a child. No iron grilles separate us from these skulls, no bossy nun dictates from her microphone. Nothing would stop you from simply reaching out and touching one. In fact, that is just what I want to do. But there is something tender and intimate here that holds me back. It is a sense not that dissimilar to the sense that prevents one invading another person's private space in conversation; and that is when I realize that something is happening to me. I am being converted. Because I cannot treat these skulls as merely objects. Fascinated as I might be by the designs, curious to turn one over in my hand and examine it, to choose another and compare the brushstrokes and the comparative talent of the generations of painters, I do not.

Light reflected from the polished metal on the opposite wall catches my eye and I look up and see myself, slightly blurred in the metal mirror. Between the real me and this fuzzy me stand ranks of skulls, the crucifix and candles, and then, reflected, the back of the cross, the back side of their heads. It seems to make the shelf of them into a small sea. They look at me and I look at them and neither of us says a thing. We can't – they are beyond language and I am without it. But I can see myself in the polished metal mirror looking at my future and my present all at once; in one inclusive moment I glimpse what I look like now and what I will be reduced to one day. Eyeless, they stare at me, their past. A swathe of time is represented in these gazes, past, present and future wrapped in one. There are lineages lined up in rows. If a present-day Ramsauer stood where I stand – or, better yet, a pregnant Ramsauer – all tenses would be there too, in a real and physical way. I am a visitor here, not related, not connected in this immediate sense, but even so I sense the reality of this connection. It is tangible. You could reach out, pick up a skull and hold this connection in your hands.

In the presence of that fragile connection I am aware of all the broken connections, as I was in Czermna. Only, where there I felt in myself hostility, here I feel compassion. There, I was faced with a wall of unresolved difference; here, with a congregation of those who have gone beyond judging. What they have done they have done; what they have left undone, is undone. That is simply a fact and they look at me with that same matter-of-factness. This is nonsense, my brain tells me. A skull is a skull; the difference can only be within me, a projection. Perhaps that is right. But it feels so different in the presence of these named skulls. It feels very much as if I am in the presence of persons.

I cannot take my eyes from all these names. Hundreds of them, clustered in families of ten or twenty. Cousins, uncles, mothers. I wonder which clusters the women came from before their names changed in marriage, whether their maiden-name skulls survey them from across the room. I wonder whether they lived in clans and factions, like Capulet and Montague. What wars and consolation are in these names I do not know. I think about the significance of names that are written – the names written in the biblical Book of Life, the names of those we love that are written in our hearts. The way that signing our name gives credit as on cheques, gives permission as in letters, or in the case of famous persons may become a souvenir.

I think of the French *souvenir*: to remember. Written in the same script, the ossuary names are almost uniform. Like a name in a register, they simply record that this person lived and died as a member of this community. Here they belong. Here they are remembered. But to those of Hallstatt who knew them, that name will carry many meanings. To one the name means tenderness, to another it means sagacity; yet another name will conjure up an image of a woman large with child, or of the old town grump.

What will my name say to those who read it when I'm gone, I wonder. And, if I had a name that described rather than merely identified me, what would it be? I think about the many names of God, and how not one of them alone is enough to describe God entirely; how these names are more like a list of qualities or attributes, or a collection of photographs from many angles. If anyone I knew stood here and looked at my name, what would it mean to them? I am not sure, and this both troubles and intrigues me. I have come a thousand miles to inspect these skulls, and I find they are quizzing me.

'What is your name?' asks the skull of Johann Baumgardner, to my left, dependable in oak leaves. 'How will you be remembered?' asks Maria Binder, beloved in roses. In the stone damp I shiver.

I do not know where to turn, where there is not a name that belongs to someone else. So I stand in the middle of the small ossuary, out of reach of any of them, without my family, without even my country or language, with my arms folded around me, and close my eyes. I wish I belonged. I wish I knew where. There, miles from anywhere I know, I really feel, deep in my bones, the ramifications of the decisions I made years ago when I left my country and went to live in another one. The deep displacement of adaptation. The thousands of losses, the thousands of assimilations by which I have become someone my childhood self would not know. Beyond that I feel, even deeper down, the strange aloneness of the human being. Naked we come into this world and naked we go out of it. Without pomp, without ceremony, accompanied by pain, and without a shred of dignity, except the simple dignity of being human. If we are not loved in the midst of this truth how can we live? I breathe in deeply. I take the air of this place down into my toes. It is not like the air in my charnel house at home. Apart from the faint scent of candle smoke, it is fresh. You can breathe safely here. If you need to, you can escape easily any time you like through a normal door with hinges. And because I can leave easily I do not need to. I stay. With my eyes closed. And I think about my name, my simple name, painted.

On the forehead of an ivory skull.
In dark blue I think, and with roses.

Definitely roses. Lush, pink garden ones, fading towards white, opulent old roses with open heads and a deep scent. They are the sort of roses you could fall into, in order to be lost, and found. When I still my considerations long enough to stop and listen to the deep wordless silence, I realize this is what I want, to be swallowed up by love, to become love – a safe place in which others may lose and find themselves again and again. Feeling alone in this small cave, I imagine my children, my friends, strangers even, falling softly into these roses, a bed of petals that is me. Falling softly and rising at will, over and over.

When I open my eyes there is this bleeding Christ, and a host of staring skulls. But I am not afraid, among the skulls, among these decorated dead.

I come back to thinking. Maybe it is because the names here are particular. Hallstatt's ossuary does not speak as Czermna did, as Sedlec did, about the ubiquity of death and the universality of mortality. These are not anyone, they are each someone, and that someone can never be me. The names tell me this: Karl Riezinger, Petrus Feldbaugh, Elizabeth Steiner, Isidor Engl. Known and identified, in a row with others who share that surname, men and women, with precise dates. They are Hallstatters. Only Hallstatters. And I am not. Maybe that is why I am not afraid.

Then too, there is colour here, and life, a kind of joy in the decorations and love in the naming. Each skull is known, is cherished or hated; at least related to another human being still alive. Their living stories and the stories of these dead intertwine in a quiet continuity of place and people that is completely unlike any of the charnel houses I have seen. Maybe that channelling of life is why I am not afraid.

Or maybe it is love: letting oneself go into the largeness of it. What did I read once? – 'by choosing a man may turn and be converted into Love.' I think there may be many such choices, such turnings, and sometimes they happen in unexpected places. I linger. Then, closing the door behind me and feeling grateful for the quiet I feel, I want to leave these Hallstatters their silence.

* * *

August was outside waiting for our impressions, and for further questions. 'This is a meeting point with mortality', he said. 'This is a confrontation. For some it is positive, for some negative. Some visitors shout and storm out of the ossuary.' Coming from the silence I was not ready for stories yet. I wanted to stay with my peace, to drink it slowly in the sunlight, without words. But August needed to tell them, and I had come to record them. I took out my notebook and pen.

He told us stories of visitors during the years he was Hallstatt's parish priest. 'One morning, at 5.30, a group of South Koreans arrived wanting to see the ossuary. I went in with them; in unison they bowed deeply and stayed quiet for two full minutes. Then they asked me to speak through an interpreter. After about half an hour they thanked me and then they got quiet again, bowed and then left in silence. It was a sacred place to them. And they were fascinated that the skulls were named. "These were people," they kept saying, "these are people, people who died."'

August continued: 'There are some Americans who have said it is all plastic. They cannot believe it would be real. Even when I tell them, "I have lived here with these people for years, I know them", they refuse to believe it.'

He told me of a mouse who had once made a home in the ossuary, several years before. One morning when he came to unlock the door he saw it shoot out of a skull's eye socket. 'She thought it was a mousehole,' laughed August, 'life and death together.' He shrugged and smiled.

I asked him whether he knew of any skulls being stolen. It had happened. Three times during his stint as priest Hallstatt skulls had arrived in the post. One of these stolen skulls, ten years earlier, had arrived with a black ribbon tied around it. At that time the neo-Nazis were involved in a campaign of postal bombing; the mayor of Vienna had had his hand blown off by one of them. So August's secretary would not allow him to open this black-ribboned parcel in the office. He opened it outside, wearing gloves, with a long pole and garden shears. Inside was a skull with a label attached written by the wife of the thief who had died without returning it. 'This skull is searching for its home and community', the message said. It is so like the story Karel told in Sedlec of the Hollywood skull that I cannot help wondering if there may be some truth in it.

'One arrived with its name bleached away', said August. The guilty thief wanted to keep anyone from knowing it belonged in Hallstatt, but it was identified by accompanying evidence. Among the Hallstatt skulls had been one of a young woman, Maria Eden, who, unlike most, had died with her teeth intact. This bleached skull arrived with a small bag of teeth accompanying it. An unnamed pupil on a school trip had stolen Maria, bleached her blank and removed all her teeth. A horrified teacher had sent the skull back. Before August placed her on the shelf next to the yellow miner, he had glued back every tooth.

Over the years dozens of Hallstatt skulls have made their way from the ossuary to museums and science labs. 'The scientists say they will return the skulls,' he said, 'but they rarely do. One laboratory tried to sell the skulls back to us. I wrote and told them "We don't buy skulls, but if you want to return them to us, we will always take them back." They never came.'

I don't know what to make of all these stories, they come so fast one after the other. August tells them straight, he tells them simply, as if they were uncomplicated facts. To me they represent a wild jumble of human reactions to death: reverence, disbelief, anger, revulsion, opportunism, guilt, regret, attempts to make amends. Each, as he tells it, is not more than an opening gambit on what could become a whole psychological discourse, none of them explored. The wildly various nature of these reactions reminds me both how deeply affected we are by the thought of mortality and how little skill we have in contemplating it. Only the animal life that shits and breeds in our disused cranial cavities seems able to remain indifferent.

* * *

Intimate and personal, Hallstatt ossuary was unlike any we had seen. More roughly hewn than any other we had encountered, it was architecturally the least complicated. There were no histories of design or restoration, no changes of ownership, and no range of architectural periods to which it belonged. It was a cave, primitive and plain, a simple repository of memory. I can see now that that is what this ossuary, this almond eye, carved in the rock face of Hallstatt is all about – remembering. Where Czermna spoke of reconciliation, and Sedlec arose out of a belief in the resurrection, what Hallstatt guards, with its simple colourful decorative naming, is the memory of its dead. It makes no attempt to build cross-cultural bridges, it makes no statement about the anonymity and ubiquity of death. It cares nothing for the dead who are not of Hallstatt. Its concern is unashamedly particular – preserving the memory of its own.

In fact, when you think about it, all of Hallstatt, from the mighty Dachstein to this humble cave, participates in the business of preserving. The mountain itself gives up, in chunks, its nautiloids and ammonites, fossils of the trapped seas its stone still remembers – salt caverns too, remainders of these past seas, and in them, preserved in his leather clothes, a man. His tools like twigs, his wizened hand memento of another age. Above the stone, beneath the ground, in Hallstatt's necropolis a thousand graves store, in posed bones, relics of a thousand people's lives. The ossuary full of names, several hundred years old, is a mere recent arrival in this field of memory.

It is easy to believe here, on the edge of this vast mountain, that we human beings matter not at all. Despite 4,000 unbroken years of human habitation, human industry and commerce, the Dachstein feels remarkably untouched. Humans have drilled holes in the mountain's side, chiselled trails, inserted pipelines, created vast caverns, perforated the limestone glacial formations by the action of iron spades and horses and eventually dynamite. We have hung our houses on the mountain's sides, tight fast as undersea anemones, rough as barnacles. With perfect composure, the mountain and the water repeat their tireless dance of permanence and transition as if we were mere bystanders. As if four thousand years of us were the blink of an eyelid. And it is. In this place of continuous human habitation and industry, we have left nothing remotely as monumental as the glaciers left when they passed through this limestone, rupturing its sides, cleaving valleys out of its adamantine interior, leaving a trail of life-bearing detritus.

Over millennia we tunnel and delve. Our kind return again and again, like deer to a salt lick, to mine and send and sell and eat this very basic commodity – salt. The mountain remains unmoved, yet all this action creates something: a civilization, a town, an empire, built on the satisfying of this primitive craving that spans all centuries and cultures of human living. It has cured our ulcers and cured our meat, flavoured our meals, preserved our provisions, cleansed our pots and polished our skin.

Salt now has 14,000 industrial, medical and domestic applications, from the manufacture of textiles to the stabilizing of boreholes from which we extract our oil. There would be no book without salt; there would be no soaps, or aluminium, or leather, or rubber. No tins, no tyres. Was there ever a time when we could live without it? Along with olive oil it was our first medicine. In the

Middle Ages it was a household's greatest treasure. The want of it still makes us poor. We taste it in our tears.

Hallstatters call it 'white gold'. Salt preserves, it heals, it enhances by drawing out the essence of a thing. Like the rocky mountainside that made the shape of sky, salt makes a thing more itself. I feel this is what the bones are doing for me. Perhaps what the preservation of human remains does for us all. When we preserve the bones of another human, known or unknown, we show them respect. Sometimes this respect is attached to their achievements or social rank, but most often it is given simply because the person was a fellow human being. When we treat human remains with respect, particularly when we treat them with respect regardless of their rank, virtue or valour, we treat ourselves with respect, for in so doing we say that humanity is one family, that 'I' and 'thou' are not in the end unrelated. What is being preserved in the charnel houses I have visited is not just those particular bones I have seen, but the beauty and dignity of being human.

If ossuaries, like salt, preserve, they can heal too, as salt can. The bone house at Czermna was all about the healing of memories and reconciliation, the redemption of remnants. And as salt brings out the flavour of things, just so do bones. Not only does facing mortality season our lives by making us realize how dear each moment is, it also invites us to consider the quality or flavour of our days, and how our days might matter. Or whether our days are lived in such a way that our life will make a difference, and if so what kind of difference that would be.

* * *

The mountains made me ask the question 'Will I be remembered?' The ossuary made me ask 'How will I be remembered?' They are each demanding questions. But the first is a question filled with existential angst; the second is a question underpinned with hope. I feel there is a kind of poetic beauty in the fact that, at Hallstatt, this second hopeful question has been literally carved out of the implacable rock that asked the first.

Memory is part of why we humans want to have children. There is love, there is the biological drive to keep one's DNA going. But there is also a need to pass on our stories, our values, our hopes, and to weave our memories into the memories of another, taking our past into the future and leaving with the next generation the memories we hold. Doing this well is not easy if you inherit a bundle of painful memories, and those who leave better memories than they carry are doing something quietly heroic, I think. Memory inheritance is a kind of signature of existence, and it doesn't only happen by parenting. Stonemasons' marks, a gardener's design, even the scraggly initials a recent flue-fitter carved at the top of our towering chimney are just such a signature. To leave no memory or to have no memory at all is in a way, one feels, to be not quite real.

In a newspaper recently I read that the Chinese are building a replica of Hallstatt on a Chinese cliff beside a Chinese lake in the province of Guandong. They have been coming to Hallstatt for years with cameras and questions, surreptitiously gleaning necessary facts and precise dimensions. They are good at such things, and I expect when it is finished one day it will be beautiful to look at. But it will have no memory.

Memory is like a shadow on the water. Falling across the flow of life it undulates, broadening and narrowing on the water's surface. The water moves but the shadow remains, a marker. Pierce it with a trout's writhing dive, smear it with the blade of a two-man kayak, it will calm again to its same wavering insistence: this is the place of the tree, the rising rock, the bare branch. Stretched even towards the engine by the wake of a boat, it will spring back true again, day after day. Such elasticity makes memory a suitable carrier of many human bonds.

We remember and are reminded at the same time. In Hallstatt where the named dead mingle with the living, a bond of memory seems real. In other parts of Europe and in the United States, and in many corners of the world, we name the resting places of our dead too, with gravestones. But there is earth between us and them, grass and soil and waste-digesting worms. We do not see a remnant of our dead. We do not handle them. At Hallstatt all of that is different. The dead are there, staring at you. And because they are named you can even stare back at your very own mum, your lavender-scented auntie, the granddad who taught you to tie your shoelace. You can touch them if you like. The connections remain somehow more tangible.

At Hallstatt, a place of deep remembering, I began to see that the memory of a person and the memory of a people are intimately linked. Proust writes of the power of memory: 'So we don't believe that life is beautiful because we don't recall it but if we get a whiff of a long-forgotten smell we are suddenly intoxicated and similarly we think we no longer love the dead because we don't remember them but if by chance we come across an old glove we burst into tears.'

These individual memories, poignant as they are, tyrannical as they can be, are by no means the only way that memory shakes and makes us. We are born into a sea of memory – familial memories, the collective memory of our tribe, the cultural memory of our people. For millions of years these evolved and grew, layer on layer, in our stories and legends, in our customs and traditions, and in our liturgies and hymns and folk songs. It is in this sea of memory that our individual memories surface like trout jumping for a light-winged fly. This pool, this sea, we take for granted – like love, when we have it, or health.

When we were, in the main, believers, our story was a story of faith with its virtues and vices and its panoply of saints, heroes and villains. What are the stories to which we now go for inspiration and instruction? They may be many and various, but it is less and less likely they are held in common. I wonder whether part of our modern sense of placelessness may have to do with the fact that our individual stories have nowhere to congregate, no family of stories of which they know themselves to be a part. My story and your story long to be part of a larger story. At Hallstatt I felt, deep in my bones, the importance of cherishing not only our individual memories, but also this sea, the memories of our peoples and our tribes.

5

Naters

As the night train rumbled towards Zürich, a sudden staccato rap on the cabin door interrupted my weary sleep; it was an abrupt wake-up call. The half-Hungarian in the bunk above, who had been tossing and turning all night, descended promptly and dressed but, despite the shaft of bright sunlight admitted to our cabin by her departure, I couldn't keep my eyes open. Fumbling about in half-light I pulled on black socks and black trousers in grey-blackness, pulled a crumpled smile from my pleasant bag and tried it on for size. It didn't fit. The official in the corridor was yelling some instruction in four languages about passports. I groaned. Zuzana told me mine was in my bag, that she had given it to me first thing. I would have sworn in a court of law that I had never seen it. But I stumbled, finally, in some semblance of order, out of the cabin into a gangway streaked with beautiful, blindingly bright sunlight. Like a mole emerging from subterranean refuge, upright and amazed, I blinked. Walensee and Zürichsee. There was sunlight on the water like sequins, and there were white paper cut-out sails.

The first things we found in Zürich station, spacious and welcoming, were the spanking-clean loos and showers – restorers of equanimity and composure. The next thing we found was our tall friend Franz, lean and familiar, who met us exactly on time in exactly the appointed place. It was Franz who had told us about Naters, a small alpine village with its charnel house where, he said, schoolchildren pass in hand-holding crocodiles to contemplate mortality. We followed, grateful, as he stowed our cumbersome bags with ease and sought out the best seats on the train which were, of course, to be found in the dining car.

Franz knew this line. He had been travelling to Brig for holidays since he was a little boy. He knew that if we sat at that very table facing in just that direction, the Swiss breakfast coming to our linen-covered table would arrive warm and welcome with an unparalleled view. And so it came, with cappuccinos and croissants, honey and ham, butter and bread and berry jam. Across the aisle I sensed the cat on a plaid cushion and her tweedy mistress mewing disapproval at this extravagance. We did not care. Like honeymooners who knew each day could never be repeated, we drank the sun, the milk, the linen and the view in satisfied and grateful gulps with greed appropriate to the perishable nature of the gift.

Outside our window, hillsides dotted with brown wooden alpine lodges glided by in swift succession. They appeared, randomly and apparently without roads leading to them, as if they had landed in the middle of grass like tossed stones. Meadows of wildflowers rose up between them, occasionally dotted with sheep. Inside, at our table, conversation turned with happy ease from travel plans to local lore. I watched, beneath my knife, the melting butter turn from creamy to clear and drip, unctuous and luxuriant, onto broken rolls. A croissant crumbled in my hand, and sunlight jewelled the berry jam. Outside field after field of wildflowers, hillside upon hillside sped past, each view, which could have merited a whole day's appreciation, receiving little more than a glance. These views so extravagantly spent, one after the other, made me feel a little drunk, as if the beauty there were inexhaustible and we possessors of a kingdom.

I leaned my elbows forward, cappuccino balanced carefully in both hands, its warm sweet nutty scent beneath my nose, and remembered what my mother used to say when I was little, calling as I carried a sliding bowl of vegetables to the family table for supper – 'use two hands'. On that moving train I wanted to hold the entire morning in both hands. It was like a life, a bright and sunny, exquisitely beautiful life, accelerated to daring speed on two sides of a window. I felt that none of it could be caught, but possibly, with two hands, some of it might be held.

At the northern tip of Thunersee sailboats leaned, peeling the blue lake silently, their pregnant sails imperfectly triangular. A motorboat varoomed a wake of white. I felt shaved, as if some layer of my self had been peeled by that boat, each moment lived was one moment less to live, each new vision also a loss, filling as it did so completely what had been a window of possibility. And time was not my friend, and gave and took too swiftly, before I had had the chance to taste, or savour, or properly delight in anything. I recalled Wordsworth's lines from his alpine tour about those 'Enticing valleys', greeted and left 'Too soon, while yet the very flash and gleam/ Of salutation were not passed away', and wished that my days too could slow to savouring speed.

Into this wish Franz unpacked his store of memories with a leisure and simplicity that seemed to take us momentarily out of time. Talking of alpine holidays in a voice that sounded far away, as if the things he was remembering – mountains and meadows, simple chalets, tilting boats – were mementoes from a distant land rather than realities just the other side of glass, I could almost forget the speed of my own journey. And then, my shoulders swayed as the train jostled, and between my fingers crumpled linen drank the almond drops of milk that spilt. Outside, in haste, hillside meadows, wild with flowers, rose again to mighty peaks. And suddenly they were upon us: the Alps.

I had never, before this charnel house tour, been to the Alps. I had hiked on lesser hills and ranges – the Poconos, the Adirondacks, the Blue Ridge Mountains, the Black Mountains, the Brecon Beacons, the Pyrenees, even the Haut Atlas – but never the Alps. And yet I felt I should know them. Alpine scenes on postcards and in advertising had made that snow-capped craggy scenery into a brand, and the Alps were, in my mind, what all mountains should look like, even though I had never stood at the foot of them. They were majestic and mighty, the mother of mountain ranges, dazzling white and justifiably proud. But they were also, in my imagination, a harsh and frightening place, for in my childhood I had heard stories of both alpine adventure and misadventure. My best friend's father had got lost mountaineering in the Alps and had survived for days by sucking water from stones. I remember the days when no one knew where he was, the international phone calls and the anxious wait. Then the awful sight of his face when he returned – peeling and red from sun exposure, his oozing lips cracked and crusted yellow, swollen and bleeding. And I remember the sheer joy in his bright blue eyes to see his family again, though it pained him terribly to look at anything because his eyes had been so badly burnt by the glacial glare. The Alps would not spare you just because you loved them. On this train, hurtling towards them, safe on the other side of glass, I wanted to forget that.

As the Jungfrau range came into view we gasped. Three peaks, rugged and fierce, gigantic and implacable, towered before us. From the velvet green of hillsides they jutted grey and harsh above their massive range – Eiger, Mönch, Jungfrau – mighty, mightier, mightiest. Regal as a company of monarchs, capped and cloaked in white with cirrus crowns and thin-stretched mists drifting along their jagged faces like blown snow, they dwarfed anything I had ever seen and certainly anything made by human hands. The Great

Wall of China, the Egyptian pyramids, the Inca remains at Cuzco; nothing we have imagined can compete for height or weight or solidity. No action we have taken can begin to compare to the colossal rending of rock that made these. Yet what we saw before us as we thundered towards Interlaken, where the southern tip of Thunersee meets its twin lake Brienzersee, was not action but magnificent and chilling stillness. Those peaks were not waiting as a waiter on a table, nor awaiting our approach. Caring nothing for us, they waited as if waiting was their reason in itself. There was nothing soft about the snow. Ice-capped stone and craggy cleft, they promised no comfort; yet all the latent Heidi in me leapt with delight. There was joy in this spectacle I did not understand, joy that was an appreciation of beauty tinged with fear and an expectation of happiness. As I write it now, I wonder whether this is what the monks and mystics seek, what makes the whirling dervish whirl – something akin to this.

That cocktail of beauty, fear and expectation seems so often to captivate and inspire us. We humans feel it when we fall in love, or take a risk on some bright future. We feel it when we set out to climb or to conquer a mountain. And what can we possibly hope to achieve on such an ascent? Even the greatest climbers make no more impact on a mountain than ants on a wall. We do not conquer mountains; the only thing we change on that ascent is ourselves. And yet from America and Europe, from China and Australia we return in thousands, by summer and winter, to visit these particular mountains: the Alps. Perhaps it is that very sense of mingled fear and awe that we seek, the draw of the vast and untameable. Maybe it is because we know we have no chance of moving them that we want to be moved by mountains. It is not only that we want to admire their beauty – in fact, mountains have not always been regarded as beautiful.

In classical times mountains might be fearsome places where one met the gods, but they were not places of beauty: meeting a god was likely to be terrifying and dangerous. The Roman poet and philosopher Lucretius had called mountain ranges 'waste places of the world'; the seventeenth-century English traveller John Evelyn, a translator of Lucretius, did not disagree. In 1646 approaching the Simplon Pass, he saw the Alps, rising after miles of even country 'as if nature had here swept up the rubbish of the Earth in the Alps, to forme and cleare the Plaines of Lombardy'. I came across Evelyn's writings again as I was reading about mountains, and across another famous seventeenth-century travel writer, the Welshman James Howell, who wrote of the Alps in a letter to his father describing them as 'Giants', 'Imposthumes' and 'Warts'. Not unlike them, the English priest and cosmographer Thomas Burnet, crossing the Simplon Pass, described the Alps in 1681 as 'wild, vast and indigested Heaps of Stone and Earth [...] the Ruins of a broken World'.

I grew up in a world already Romanticized, but to those educated in the Neoclassical tradition in which beauty and truth were related to proportion, symmetry, regularity and order, the Alps appeared at once monstrous and engrossing. Howell and Evelyn were appalled and enthralled at the same time; their alpine tour challenged their whole notion of order and beauty. Looking back at them looking forward, we can see that the precipices they negotiated were not purely physical cliffs of stone and ice, that the fear and thrill of their alpine crossings intimated modernity's exchange of security for possibility. It was a shift that took hundreds of years to complete.

Two hundred years after those early alpine adventurers, and with a radically different take on beauty which violated those Classical canons of symmetry and proportion, the Romantic poets of the nineteenth century like Shelley, Byron and Wordsworth found a fierce pleasure in the irregularity of Nature. And John Ruskin, who devoted almost half of his book *Modern Painters* (1843) to discussing attitudes to mountains in painting and poetry, saw mountains as a root of joy. Admitting that this was something new, he imagined that a person of his generation unaccustomed to this penchant for mountains in landscape would enter a gallery and think, 'There is something strange in the minds of these modern people! Nobody ever cared about blue mountains before, or tried to paint the broken stones of old walls.'

Reading Marjorie Hope Nicolson's study of the sublime and the infinite, *Mountain Gloom and Mountain Glory*, I found that she notes this too: the Greeks had been interested in men, horses, birds; the Medievals had used a rough attempt at rock merely to divide light behind a human figure, but in Western art the landscape had never before been itself the subject. Something in the previous two centuries had rent the ordered fabric of beauty, and that thing, that culture-shifting projectile, was the thrilling experience of terror. In fact Nicolson would assert that 'terror' became an integral part of the new aesthetic. This really interests me, because terror has been so much a part of my journey into bones and I have wondered how it can be that something so terrible to look at can also be thought beautiful. The early alpine travel writers, although they do not explain it, have charted this anomaly.

John Dennis, one of the first to publish his alpine travels (*Miscellanies*, 1693), described how his new alpine experience gave him a delight that was not consistent with reason; it was 'mingled with Horrours, and sometimes almost with despair'. None of it made sense: he felt 'a delightful Horrour, a terrible Joy' and, as he walked along craggy cliffs or peered down cutting chasms at the very brink of death, he confesses that 'at the same time that I was infinitely pleas'd I trembled'. Similarly Joseph Addison, returning from his Grand Tour, wrote that 'The Alps fill the mind with an agreeable kind of horror', and he began to make a distinction between 'the beautiful' and 'the sublime' that was developed further by Edmund Burke.

In these writers I find that my fledgling experience of mingled terror and beauty, or something like it, has been recorded before, and not only recorded but eventually understood. In Burke's *Ideas of the Sublime and the Beautiful* (1756), horror plays a large part in moving one towards the sublime. The imagination is moved to awe by what is 'dark, uncertain and confused'; fear and attraction are felt together in an inexplicable draw towards what is unknown and infinite. Philosophers such as Kant, Hegel and Schopenhauer followed with their own developments on the theme. All the raw material of the early alpine travellers of the seventeenth century began to take a new shape as the nineteenth-century aesthetic theory developed to one in which beauty was regular, symmetric and proportional while the sublime was ragged or rough, uneven, awe-inspiring, even terrifying. It makes sense that, by the time Wordsworth, Shelley and Byron came to write their poems, the crude and monstrous in nature had become a savage and solemn majesty.

What intrigues me further about all of this is that it takes me back to Thoreau, whose wish to live simply and deliberately and to face the essential facts of life inspired my journey into bones because, a few decades after Wordsworth and Shelley were writing in England, Thoreau started exploring the great face of nature in America in his own search for the sublime. When he built his rough-hewn cabin at Walden Pond in 1845 and decided to devote two years, two months and two days of his life to living in the greatest simplicity he could imagine, he chose a humble life he loved; but he was frustrated too by the relative tameness of Walden Pond, and ventured on excursions into greater wilderness that still could not satisfy his hunger for the awful wild. Even at the summit of Mount Kataddin in Maine, he found himself craving a greater experience of wildness than his tours of Maine and Cape Cod afforded. It was as though the small and local life was somehow nourished by the magnificent and majestic. I wonder what he would have made of the Alps. I would so like to have seen him at Hallstatt, approaching the top of the Salzberg, before the tourists had got there. I would like to have seen him cutting through the Simplon Pass.

* * *

Past bustling Interlaken and pretty Kandersteg, a small charming town with a stone bridge arching across its tumbling stream, our last stretch of the journey to Naters was by bus. Flat green playing-fields stretched either side of the road at the outskirts of town. Beyond these there were white stone houses with balconies and shutters at the windows, arranged in irregular streets rising gradually towards the centre. Above them on the hillside, houses were built right against the mountainside, their terraced gardens approached via long, steep and sometimes switchback staircases. Higher still the mountains rose, to first treeless and then snow-dusted and finally glacial peaks.

Down here at the base of the village, on these playing-fields that seemed to be the only flat parcel of land the village had, fitness enthusiasts in bright Lycra outfits gathered in classes of a dozen or so facing their instructors. They all appeared to be carrying ski poles. In summer. And then, as one group struck off behind its instructor in great loping strides, I realized they were not ski poles at all but walking sticks, and that these were classes for alpine hikers. How seriously they took their preparations. I had always considered a bottle of water and a muesli bar to be preparation enough; clearly I knew nothing about the Alps.

In bright sunlight and in heat that was surprisingly intense, we disembarked near the centre of town and met without difficulty our expert guide who was going to be able to answer every question we might have on the Naters charnel house. Several questions were already penned in my notebook, with spaces beneath them left blank for his answers. But he did not take us to the charnel house. Instead we passed through tree-lined avenues and up intriguing lanes, stopped before historic doorways and beneath the balconies of previous local worthies. 'Where is the charnel house?' I asked, my hand shading my eyes as we looked up to view, at the spot where he recalled the courtship of a local hero, a balcony of pretty but inconsequential tumbling pelargoniums. 'Are we nearly there?'

We trudged on. It was never far. We were always on the way, but the notebook wilted in my hands as we were shown the baroque treasures of yet another parish church. It wasn't that these were ugly or boring or in any way inadequate. In fact, given unlimited time I felt I would have wanted to linger and admire them, but we had crossed five countries to see something quite different. He was not happy to have his requisite fee paid, in cash, at the foot of the town hall steps; he did not think he deserved it since his tour was only half given. I would have paid him double for a quarter of his time.

At last the bones that were calling me, or at least the chapel beneath which they lay, came into view. Down a narrow cobbled street flanked by white houses with grey stone corners, we spied its slate-roofed bell tower topped with a shiny cross. As we walked towards it, short stone staircases led up to the front doors of houses whose bright pots of flowers stood on their steps like liveried sentries. Then, just opposite the church of St Mauritius, a small, cobbled piazza opened out. There stood the little chapel, taking up not much more ground than a two-roomed cottage, though taller and towered, with its *Beinhaus* below; its white walls and stone corners just like all the other houses; its above-street-level doors, like theirs, reached by a double stone staircase rising from the street at either side.

Below the stairs, directly beneath the chapel doors, a simple arch, like half a moon, rose from out of the cobbles at one end and sank into them again at the other. This arch roughly marked the ceiling line of the *Beinhaus* whose floor was well below ground. A wooden bench was fitted across this arch, and the opening to the undercroft below was filled with a heavy iron grille so that the *Beinhaus* bones, though easily visible as you looked through and down, remained entirely out of reach. Nevertheless, said the bench and the two dozen red votive candles that were lit and laid along the stone sill of the charnel house, you are invited to linger here. To pray, or ponder, or to remember. Sighing, that is just what we did. The bench beneath the arch was in the shade, and the stone wall behind my back was delightfully cool. It was a comfortable place to be. There was time, and no rushing. And so we waited.

Three young teenagers just out of school with rucksacks on their backs glanced at the bones as they passed. Once past the arch, they ran around to the back of the stone steps urgently, as if in a game of hide-and-seek. When the coast was clear they left, smacking each other's palms in a high-five. A boy on his bike, sweatshirt hanging loose from his head by its hood, rolled gently by, jacket flapping behind him like a habit, then once beyond the piazza he stood on his pedals and zoomed. A young man on his motorbike killed his speed at the charnel arch, and revved it up again on the other side. What was it they saw that slowed them down? Or was it what they felt?

I turn, and peering through the grille I sense it too. Though not at first. At first I only notice bones stacked one upon another as in many other charnel houses. A wall of bones that must be 12 feet

high and at least twice as wide, mostly skulls, fills the entire side of
the undercroft opposite the grille. Here at Naters they are stacked
with femurs between the skulls, so that the cranium above, which
has lost its jaw, will have something on which to rest and thus stay
upright; but the effect is to make each skull look as it if it is spewing
the knuckle end of a femur out of its mouth. Or as if it is gagging
on bones.

As I have learned to do so often on this tour, I retreat from the
edge of horror into the safety of facts: technically these are crania,
not skulls, for they have lost their mandibles. And then, to secure my
safe position, I pile into my mind more of the odd little bits of information that I have picked up on my journey into bones, such as that
a skull is really a whole system of bones – eight cranial and 14 facial –
and that the sutures by which they are connected occur nowhere else
in the body; or that it takes seven different bones to form the cavity in
which an eye rests and that this cavity is also called an 'orbit', which,
like the path of the earth itself, is also an imperfect circle.

My head carries more facts than it did when I began this journey.
Words like 'viscerocranium' and 'neurocranium' make sense to me,
and I know that over half of the 206 bones in my entire body are in
my hands and feet. My familiarity with bones and its concomitant
accumulation of facts has not bred contempt, but it can render
this charnel house less shocking. Displacing the choking and
spewing images, I view the cranial curves with a certain degree
of detachment. I am not appalled by the number of them, or the
brutality of their separation from the rest of their skeletons. I am
not frightened by the evil portent of their unblinking stares, the
empty holes of noses long gone. I am hardly even curious about the
stories suggested by the occasional abnormality of an old cranial
wound. By now I have seen all of these a dozen times over. There
are no terrors here.

And yet my fingers wrap themselves securely around the fat round bars that run horizontally and vertically to form the regular squares of the iron grille. Cold to my touch, they are here, I know, to protect the heads from me, or some rogue like me, alive and breathing and maybe in addition drunk, who might not resist the urge to batter, paint, scratch, smash, or remove remaining teeth. Or who might imagine, as I have just done, the awful possibility of bringing the whole wall down upon himself by yanking out a few heads from the bottom. The remains of an estimated 30,000 people, more than three times the number of Naters's living residents, have been dumped behind this neat and tidy wall and all of that, too, would come tumbling down upon the miscreant in one clattering wave of death. Just as there is a strong urge to preserve the contents of an ossuary, so there has always been an opposite urge to deface and destroy them. I discovered while researching for this book that across Europe, from Portugal to Austria and beyond, through neglect and sometimes through malicious intent, charnel houses have become tool sheds, tobacco stores or even manure dumps, skulls have been defaced, de-toothed and sometimes stolen. And this is not necessarily the result of modern contempt or social delinquency – graffiti has been noted in various places from the seventeenth and eighteenth centuries; one skull at a charnel house in Portugal carries, it is claimed, the autograph of Alexandre Dumas. So it is not at all an idle thought that some rogue could come one day and send the whole wall at Naters tumbling.

The chapel above is still used for funerals – in fact there is a coffin there now and someone moving benches and preparing flowers – but the Naters ossuary does not have opening hours. Sheltered but not totally enclosed, it is open to passers-by and to the vagaries of weather, and this openness seems to be a large part of what allows it to be an integrated part of local life. But it also renders the ossuary bones more vulnerable than in other places. I understand the need not only for the roof, but also for the grille and for the spiked iron railings that enclose the bones yet further inside the undercroft itself.

As I lay my hot, sun-drenched cheek against the cool iron bars and gaze at this wall of bones, I feel no terror or alarm, but a kind of weariness and something that feels like resignation. It is as if I have stopped fighting, or running. As if I have been found. There is a naked man pinned to a plank of wood mounted directly in front of the wall of skulls. An implausibly bright gilded cloth covers his loins. Knotted at the side, it flaps out as if caught by some breath of wind. But there is no wind, no stirring air at all, and just one breath or two perhaps left in him. Blood trickles from his temple across his rugged cheekbones to his beard, and at his feet and hands little red rivers make maps of his extremities. His ribs, his knees and all the sinews of his arms, the tendons in his neck, the curves of his fingers clenched in towards the bloody palms: all these exert themselves in one last expense of energy. He is beautiful and bare and terrible to look at, there in front of that death wall, dying. Always dying and never dead. And they, brutally bald behind him, remain, their eyeless orbits staring, speechless with their jawless mouths. On either side of him two companions stand, a woman and a man, his mother and his friend, clothed, appalled and mute.

There are no guides or guidebooks here, no trinkets for sale. Not even a single weathered leaflet. All that can be said is said in bleached bone and by that life-sized gilded statue, and then there is silence. The running has stopped. So has the fear. I sit and listen to my breathing, feel the iron bars cold against my fingers, the cool stone firm against my shoulder. My ankles in the sun feel drenched in liquid gold. Beside me several candles that have been lit hours earlier – this morning maybe, before the schoolchildren and the motorbike passed – flicker still in their tall red jars.

I wonder what fingers have touched the spent matches that lie like dried black worms on the white stone ledge. I wonder about the lives attached to those fingers, and how much of them is spent, and whether or not they have begun to be lived at all. And only then I notice the words, the first words this place has offered, there above the statue and the bones. Words that are gilded, like his loincloth; that run across the length of the bone wall in German gothic, gold on a black wood beam, upright and firm. Even before I decipher the translation I can see that these are not words to be trifled with: *Was ihr seid, das waren wir/ Was wir sind, das werdet ihr.* 'What you are, we were/ What we are, you shall be.'

It is a phrase so perfectly balanced that it makes me slightly giddy to look at, as if it could tip at any moment on its fulcrum of *wir* and *Was*, of 'we' and 'what', so that the fact becomes the question and 'what we are' turns into 'what are we?' Swirling gold on black, the words wrap back upon themselves, innocent as doves and smooth as serpents: 'What you are, we were/ What we are, you shall be.' There is no gainsaying this mirror phrase. It is like the other mirror here: the dead beneath them, who are the most uninviting mirror I have ever looked at. For I see here, with my cheek against the grille, with my face leaning absolutely as close as it can to these terrible images, that I am no longer looking, as I did in other charnel houses, at the macabre dead, at an interesting piece of political or social history, or at an artist's installation. I am, finally, looking at myself.

Whereas the dead at Czermna had frightened me and the dead at Sedlec had puzzled me, where all of the places I had visited had intrigued me and informed me, here at Naters I am simply stopped. The dead at Hallstatt had had a power to speak to me because they were known dead, named and loved; they were people. Here the dead, despite being nameless, are so intimate beneath their chilling motto as to be a mirror to that most familiar of all things: the self.

They are not only human like us, they *are* us. They are a prophecy of our unavoidable future.

* * *

Between the roof of the house opposite and the eave of the chapel a craggy alpine peak is framed, white-capped and angular, against a deep blue sky. It is not so much majestic to me from this angle as simply present and solid, immovable as a fate. Or, more hopefully, a destiny. I cannot help reflecting that this village, Naters, at the foot of the Simplon Pass is so near where all those early alpine travellers passed. They crossed the mountains I am only approaching, facing death, and strange and startling beauty, at every turn. It is not possible to follow in their tracks. Not really; not the interior tracks that took them from security through horror to the sublime at every precipice. In the decades that followed them, roads and bridges reduced the perils, and fashion replaced adventure. A real sense of horror could not remain, partly because the very writings that had encouraged others to follow had also made the journey familiar. Thirty years after Wordsworth's first crossing of the Simplon Pass he visited again, noting that pilgrims of fashion hurried along discussing the merits of the latest novel, poring over guidebooks, or even fast asleep; the peculiar blend of terror and beauty experienced by those early travellers that engendered our whole notion of the sublime had largely passed.

Twenty-three-year-old Thomas Gray, of 'Elegy in a Country Churchyard' fame, wrote of his alpine tour in a letter to a friend: 'You have Death perpetually before your eyes, only so far removed as to compose the mind without frightening it.' Most of the cliffs from which I might have fallen on my journey so far have been psychological ones. Yet, passing here where early alpine travellers had their famous first encounters with the sublime, and with death perpetually before my eyes as it has been during the length of this tour, I wonder whether something of what I have felt – horror and beauty, fear and awe – is akin to their forays into a new sublime. I do feel myself to be at the edge of something strangely beautiful. Looking outward from this edge is the pull of the sublime. But looking inward, I am not sure I would call it the sublime – it feels too small and personal for that; something maybe more like humility, although as soon as I mention the word I feel embarrassed. I want to erase that, go back and use another word.

How do you even begin to talk about humility? No one wants to name it or own it, or even look at it. We favour celebrity and power, fame and success, but from humility we collectively, instinctively and unanimously avert our eyes. It sounds too much like humiliation, which most of us at some point in our lives have experienced, and which we fear. It does not equip us for survival let alone for success. Not only is it deeply unfashionable, we feel the pursuit of it could be actually detrimental. In fact Aristotle, in his writing on the virtues, considered too much of it a vice, and it is not only ancient philosophers who have denigrated humility; Nietzsche reminds us of the impossible irony that whoever humbles himself 'wishes to be exalted'. Any talk of humility seems like a hiding to nothing. And yet, as Stephen Cherry notes in his recent book *Barefoot Disciple*, humility may have something to offer the modern world. The modern French philosopher, atheist and best-selling author André Comte-Sponville rates humility as a 'great virtue', eighth in his list of eighteen, and the philosopher and novelist Iris Murdoch called it the central virtue, though a 'rare and unfashionable' one. Around it, she believed, other virtues can be integrated into a sovereign good.

This is small comfort to me. I am still left dreading the word, for to write about humility is either to be seen as proud for pretending to know something about it, or oppressive. We simply do not believe that humility can be either real or good. In spite of that, 'humility' is the word that keeps coming back to me, faithful as a dog. I do not even know what I mean by it. Dictionaries tell me that it means being meek and respectful, having a modest estimate of one's own importance; that it signifies lowliness or submissiveness.

Looking at those unnumbered bones I sense that this definition, though it feels familiar, may be only half the picture and that, while humility certainly involves regarding limits, what is most important, most liberating about it is that it involves being real. I like what Comte-Sponville says about humility, that it is based in honesty: 'Being humble means loving the truth and submitting to it. Humility means loving truth more than oneself.' I want to love truth. In particular, among other things, I want to love the truth that, although our limitations are real, so also are the joys of our ordinary days. As Cherry puts it, 'genuine attempts to describe humility, and honest efforts to live humbly, point us away from fantasy and towards reality. They bring us down to earth. Humility is the *earthiest* of virtues. It is not about being pious; it is about being grounded.'

If exploring humility is exploring the reality of the ordinary then humility, like its linguistic cousin *humus*, is the product of long, slow and earthy change. Maybe I do know what I mean by the word humility after all. Or at least why the word won't clear off, no matter how many times I shoo it away. I sense, in that moment, sitting there with the cool stone of the Naters ossuary at my back and the fierce Swiss sunlight tingling on my calf (and with a strange kind of shyness, as if I am shy even of myself), at once the smallness and the greatness of one human life.

This kind of humility, a humility of the real and the grounded, of the honest and the true, is something I can honestly, openly and wholeheartedly seek. And I can do so believing that, like its cousin humus, it will provide a rich and sustaining place for roots. There is a kind of normality here at the charnel house in Naters, an ordinariness about life and about death. As if there is death in life and life in death. That's a simple truth, and easier to bear, perhaps, on a sunny day in the first burst of summer, and in the company of friends.

* * *

The charnel house at Naters states so clearly what in fact all the charnel houses have been saying. Here it is written in gold, succinct and unavoidable: I will be, like that, ash-white bone. I need the unflinching simplicity of that reality check because, like the vast majority of North Americans, I was brought up quite unconsciously in an atmosphere that denied death and that denial has stayed with me despite the loss of several people I have loved. There have been church funerals and family funerals, with real tears and heavy sobs; yet when the tears subside, the reality of death seems for me to subside with them.

The first funeral I remember was not a funeral at all but a 'thanksgiving service' for a twinkly-eyed old gentleman who was the metaphorical grandfather of the congregation of the Independent Bible church to which my family belonged. I wore the rather ugly bright yellow skirt I had just made in my seventh grade Home Economics class and a white cotton blouse embroidered with yellow-centred daisies – we were not to wear black and weep as those who had no hope. Of course we knew that lovely old George Quell had died, that his genial laugh would not be heard in the entrance hall among the snow-shedding winter coats, that the flow of bright shiny sweets in cellophane wrappers that slipped like jewels from his palm into our jubilant fingers had abruptly ceased, and that the big child in him would no more wink at us indulgently across a room of grown-ups. This we knew; but what we *did* was celebrate. Or rather pretend no grief. Not as children pretend – but a grown-up pretending in which you did something imaginary that was not fun.

What we knew and what we did separated like the long peel of an apple which, even when it is peeled expertly in one long single curl, cannot ever be put back exactly right. We all did this, children and grown-ups alike. I felt wrong as I walked up the long aisle to view him, unnaturally suntanned and coiffed in his coffin; stood there in my yellow skirt garish as the trumpet of a municipal daffodil. I was shocked by the unfamiliarity of his so-familiar face and stunned by the cunning stealth of some hand that had removed not only him but also the memory of his real face from my mind, and replaced it with a lying 'memory photo' which only half-smiled without the twinkle. This invisible hand too, I knew, as I processed back to my seat, was also stealing my tears, locking them up in the vault in which unsuitable things must live out their lives wrangling like starved hyenas. In other parts of life 'know' and 'do' could be harmonious, but not here, not in death. In death they separated irretrievably.

I do not think the religion that surrounded this ceremony was the primary reason for this divorce. The Christian hope to which George Quell had adhered in life – that is, that in death, he would live again – certainly fed the notion that his death was not an unmitigated tragedy. But this particular denial of death, or rather this refusal to grieve, could be performed so unquestioningly and with such candour because it participated in the wider death denial that so insidiously shapes the prevailing contemporary American consciousness.

Other Christian cultures and many other religions allow their members to grieve, to wail, even in some places to perform outlandish displays of mourning. At a Greek Orthodox funeral, widows in black will drape themselves over coffins wailing dirges for hours, men will bow and kiss the coffin or a cross, and women may faint with grief. Or in Sicily on the Day of the Dead and in Brittany on the Feast of All Souls, relatives will take food to the graveyard and place it on the graves of their family members, because the dead are not anathema. But in America denial of death is a cultural mainstay. It has become part of our very identity, or at least who we imagine we are: the people who do not die. We are invincible in weaponry, intrepid in battle, superior in military intelligence; we develop the latest treatments for illness, discover electricity, the telephone, the atom bomb. We fly to the moon and claim it with a flag. The moon.

Add to this cocktail of bombastic confidence the funeral indus-try's trend against plain talking, and it is not hard to see how death has become not only unspeakable but also unbelievable. In fact, completely unreal. Perhaps the best thing to do is let the death industry speak for itself on the subject, which is exactly what Jessica Mitford did in her groundbreaking 1963 study *The American Way of Death* which chronicles the growth of the funeral industry through the twentieth century in North America. She notes that, just as in Dale Carnegie's 'lexicon of the successful man there is no such word as "failure", so have the undertakers managed to delete the word "death" from their vocabularies'.

This has not been accidental. Over the years there have been various guides published to indicate which words were 'in' and which were 'out'. As early as 1916 glossaries substituted 'prepare body' for 'handle corpse' but, as noted in the updated version of Mitford's book, instructions about correct usage have evolved so that, today, even 'body' is out. A whole deathless vocabulary has emerged in which the person's name is substituted for 'body' or 'corpse', there is a 'service' rather than a 'funeral', a 'preparation room' rather than a 'morgue', a 'vital statistics form' rather than a 'death certificate' (as if anything was 'vital' in the dead – vitality is precisely what they lack). The grave is 'opened' and 'closed' like a door, not 'dug' and 'filled' like a hole. The body is not 'buried' but 'interred'. There is certainly no 'graveyard' or even a 'cemetery' but a 'memorial park'. Pre-purchased plots are sold as 'pre-use memorial estates' as if they were a property investment. A person is 'deceased' not 'dead' because they have not 'died', but 'expired'. And so they need 'clothing' instead of a 'shroud'.

In fact, there are whole catalogues of clothing especially manufactured for corpses. Mitford famously notes the 'Fit-a-Fut Oxford' which comes in patent, tan or oxblood with an open back so the shoe can be slipped easily onto a rigor mortis foot. The Practical Burial Footwear Company of Columbus, Ohio also sells the 'Ko-Zee' with, as Mitford notes, 'soft, cushioned soles and warm, luxurious slipper comfort, but true shoe smartness'. Ethel Maid Inc. of Schuykill Haven, Pennsylvania, who have been making corpse clothing since 1931, dress the dead in all the layers of the living. For ladies there is everything from panties, hose, vests and slips to negligées, dresses and even lace gloves. For men there is a choice of athletic shorts, boxers or briefs, robes and pyjamas or a range of suits. Was he a boxers man or a briefs man? Is he now asleep or dressed to impress?

Once dressed, the next question is how comfortable will the mattress in the coffin be. We are assured that the 'Beautyrama adjustable Soft-Foam Bed' is 'soft and buoyant, but will hold firm without slipping'. The Batesville Casket Company offer many styles of boxes in wood options from cherry and mahogany to walnut and maple, oak, pecan and pine; or you can go the extra mile and have solid nickel or titanium named 'Anthem Silver' and 'Renaissance Rose', although what is sung in the nickel and what is 'Renaissance' about titanium remains to be seen.

In this strange bereavement dialect, what parades as delicacy is in fact a kind of bullying; in unfamiliar territory and often in a shaken state, you are steered by soft voices into parting with vast sums of money to the benefit of no one you love. What feels like deference is manipulation. The expression of the real is circumscribed at every turn by silky prohibitions that are deliberately cultivated to forbid frankness and to avoid straightforward questions a child might ask, like 'If he is dead, why does he need comfortable shoes?' These forbidden words are commercially as well as psychologically significant; the beneficiaries of this scheme are certainly not the bereaved.

What concerns me more than an undertaker's understandable desire to make a profit, however, is the way in which this relentless sidestepping of death has stolen our words. More lamentable than the loss of monetary millions is the corporate loss of language, and with it the means to express thoughts and emotions freely. The insidious nature of scripted talk means that its prohibitions begin to guide our thinking (after all, it is how the professionals speak) so that, even in our own homes among family and friends, we often feel constrained by false delicacy in our conversations about death. In the last hundred years public discourse has evolved so that we have effectively excised the vocabulary of death from common parlance. Except as an attempted joke, like that line from the comedian Woody Allen: 'I am not afraid of death; I just don't want to be there when it happens.'

America may lead the vanguard of death denial, but the United States is not the only culture in which the denial of death has made headway. In fact, as Paul Koudounaris points out in his recent study of charnel houses, *The Empire of Death*, a gradual alienation from death has been going on for centuries in much of Western society. As early as the sixteenth and seventeenth centuries our dialogue with the dead, and the speech about death that was a normal part of life throughout the Middle Ages, began to grow silent. It was not only the advances of medicine, by which we came to associate contamination and disease with the dead, that banished it, but also our new human identity as independent 'selves' that had evolved with the Enlightenment. Where once identity was found in the corporate and communal, it came to be found in the individual. Now we are our bodies and our limit is our skin; death, as an irreducible and unequivocal state, has become a boundary rather than a transition. And the denial of death goes on finding new means of expression.

The writer and former professor John Gray's recent book *The Immortalisation Commission* traces the modern quest to cheat death, as the search for eternal life left the realms of religion and moved into the laboratory. He points to the early psychical researchers who, reacting against Darwinism which saw humans as another kind of beast, attempted to demonstrate immortality through séances. These were not mere kooks but some of the most eminent persons of their day. In Britain nineteenth-century Spiritualism named among its followers the novelist Sir Arthur Conan Doyle, the co-discoverer of Darwinism Alfred Russel Wallace, the Cambridge philosopher Henry Sidgwick and the Nobel-prize-winning physiologist Charles Richet. A British Prime Minister, Arthur Balfour, was also President of the Society for Psychical Research which sought to examine paranormal events 'in an unbiased and scientific way'. Some of these researchers believed they were conducting, through thousands of pages of automatic writing over thirty years, the work of dead scientists, speaking from the afterlife to bring peace to this world. In a mixture of science and the occult that was meant, according to Gray, to replace religion, science was drawn into an attack on science.

Not content in its pursuit of the implausible, modern Western society carried on in the twentieth century with further attempts to cheat death through sciences such as cryonics and singularity. *The Prospect of Immortality* by Robert Ettinger, published in 1964, became the bible of cryonics; and it needed a bible, because cryonics is not only about living forever, but also about living better. It is not only about preservation and resuscitation, but about ridding ourselves of the imperfections of life and about raising us above the level of beasts. Ettinger claims 'we will remould, nearer to the heart's desire, not just the world but ourselves'. Those resuscitated 'will be not only revived and cured but enlarged and improved'.

As the psychical research of the nineteenth century rejected Darwinism's logical conclusion that humans are simply beasts, so does cryogenics. Alan Harrington's cryogenic text *The Immortalist: An Approach to the Engineering of Man's Divinity* describes the cryonic project as 'a demand to be rescued from nothingness'. He writes: 'Only by subduing the processes that force us to grow old will we be able to exempt ourselves from death, the lot of beasts.' Cryonics is not simply an American freak show; there are cryonic associations now in the United Kingdom and a growing industry among the newly wealthy of Russia.

Another attempt at immortality, espoused by the American visionary Ray Kursweil, is the theory of Singularity in which humans will transcend biology through the application of artificial intelligence. According to this theory, nanotechnology will enable the development of nanobots, or molecular robots, that will reverse ageing and enhance the activities of the brain, resulting in a fusion of human and artificial intelligence. We will cease to be biological organisms, with our 'nano-engineered bodies far more capable and durable than our biological human bodies'. We will live mainly outside the material world in virtual environments.

These modern theories seem to many as weird as the psychical research of the nineteenth century, and even if they materialized there is no promise that surviving under such conditions would be desirable. Supposing cryonics actually worked – in what sort of a world might you wake up? Would it be a world that wanted you, or treated you as a slave, or a parasite? Would there be a stable government and laws? Not only do these emerging theories of immortality rely on the steadiness and hospitality of a future world, neither of which can be predicted, they also rely on the existence of human institutions which, as Gray notes, are inescapably mortal.

Whereas it is often said that science was born in the rejection of superstition, Gray argues that it was instead born in the rejection of absolute rationalism. Science relies on observation and experiment and the results of these are, he reminds us, accepted even when what they suggest seems impossible. At the bottom of scientific attempts to defeat death is the larger attempt to escape chaos, but there is no escape from either contingency or mystery. We will always be subject to chance and surrounded by the unknowable.

One thing we do know: we will in fact die. Defer it though we may, we cannot in the end avoid it. Wouldn't it be better to look that short fact straight in the face now and let its reality burn the dross from our days? Thoreau said it like this:

> If you stand right fronting, and face to face to a fact, you will see the sun glimmer on both its surfaces, as if it were a cimeter, and feel its sweet edge dividing you through the heart and marrow, and so you will happily conclude your mortal career. Be it life or death, we crave only reality. If we are really dying, let us hear the rattle in our throats and feel cold in the extremities; if we are alive, let us go about our business.

It seems to me that here at the Naters charnel house, where you can visit the dead almost accidentally, that is what people do. They go about their business aware of a stark inevitability most of us attempt to avoid. I am told that Naters primary schoolchildren have been walked to the charnel house in a crocodile of neat pairs to view the bones as part of their ordinary school week. Whether you walk past, stop and light a candle or just slow down your motorbike, the dead are not alien here – at least not here in this small courtyard. I wonder whether it makes any difference to their lives, this wake-up call in their midst. Proust believed that the threat of death had the power to enliven your days, but that we mostly forget about mortality again and need to be reminded. He wrote:

> I think that life would suddenly seem wonderful to us if we were threatened to die as you say. Just think of how many projects, travels, love affairs, studies, it – our life – hides from us, made invisible by our laziness which, certain of a future, delays them incessantly. But let all this threaten to become impossible for ever, how beautiful it would become again! Ah! If only the cataclysm doesn't happen this time, we won't miss visiting the new galleries of the Louvre, throwing ourselves at the feet of Miss X, making a trip to India. The cataclysm doesn't happen, we don't do any of it, because we find ourselves back in the heart of normal life, where negligence deadens desire. And yet we shouldn't have needed the cataclysm to love life today. It would have been enough to think that we are humans, and that death may come this evening.

There is one man at least at Naters who claims his life has been enhanced by a daily reminder of mortality. We met him as we were standing by the charnel house looking up at the steel snowguards that run like trolley-lines across the roof slates. He strolled up to the charnel house arch and stopped. Stephen Petrus, a tall, lean man with an old army injury and a loping stride, who wore his pain like a garment, familiar and visible. His lower right arm and hand that had been wrapped in cloth and supported in a sling for the last thirty-five years was what you saw at first glance. About the other painful events in his life he made no particular disclosures though they surfaced nevertheless between the words that tumbled out of him, intriguing and oblique, like footnotes to a soliloquy on which he embarked with little hesitation.

He spoke with courage and without the normal inhibitions that would prevent one offering philosophical views to utter strangers. There was an intensity and a warmth in his greeting that made it impossible not to engage with him, even though his eyes were a little too penetrating for comfort and his breath carried on it the scent of a midday glass of wine. He loved the *Beinhaus*. He came here every day, even in winter, to read its inscription and visit its people, because it was here that he was put in touch again and again with his interior life.

'How does coming here change your life?' I asked him. It doesn't convert you to being Catholic, he insisted. It wasn't about being good but about being real, about not pretending anything. 'The meaning of life', he said, leaning slightly like a pine in the wind, 'is in the not knowing what will be after you die. Not knowing *is* the meaning because it makes you rely on grace.'

People look for meaning in fun, he told us, but meaning is found only in giving. You should give yourself as a present, without expectation of return. 'Whenever you give yourself as a present you get it ten times back. Having fun is ultimately meaningless. It doesn't bring you anywhere because it is a repetition – you go in a circle.' And then he pointed to the stones in front of him, the earth and the bones. 'The meaning is here', he said. And then he looked over his shoulder at that gold inscription. 'We want to know what will be. The meaning is not in knowing what will be in the afterlife, but in knowing this is how *I* will be. What I feel in the morning when I wake up is this awareness inside. This awareness is God present with me.'

I sensed that Stephen Petrus had little concern for creeds. 'Whether you say you believe or not does not matter', he asserted. 'This place, this connects me to the subconscious. What comes out of you is what matters – not the ideas to which you assent. The deep part of you is the same whether you believe or don't believe – it is the same for everybody. You don't always think about what you do, but you act from what comes from inside you.'

His words came fast and forcefully, so fast that it took Franz and Zuzana translating in tandem to accommodate the cataract of thoughts and, though my brain sent its messages to my pen with great alacrity, my pages, when I came to view them later, were a mass of scribbles and crossings out, arrows and brackets. We listened with the sun hot on our backs, we listened as again and again he talked of love and pain, and the need for acceptance. The shadows had moved from overhead to the side of the charnel house, becoming long again before he had spent his words. 'It doesn't play a part what church you belong to,' he said at last, as a sliver of shade greyed the stark white corner of my notebook, 'what matters is that you look inside yourself. That you do *hear* the voice inside you. That you do hear what you need. That you simply *can* hear this voice is what matters. You need grace whether you believe or not. You are weak; and when you know it then you are *demütig*, you are humble.'

* * *

Wordsworth made his alpine journey in the late spring and summer of 1790. In the *Prelude* he records how he entered narrow chasms flushed with rushing streams past 'stationary blasts of waterfalls', chased along torrents where 'brook and road were fellow-travellers', through narrow rents and 'black drizzling crags' not unlike those we had descended at Hallstatt. Giddy and sick with the height of the drop and with 'the tumult and peace, the darkness and the light' which ran together like workings of a single mind or 'features of the same face', he sensed 'the symbols of Eternity – first, and last, and midst, and without end'. This brush with timelessness, the feeling of his own smallness in the vast heights and depths of the alpine peaks and crags was for him not paralysing but invigorating. The Alps stirred in him 'an under-thirst/ Of vigour seldom utterly allayed'. Crossing the Simplon Pass and passing through the Alps not so far from Naters, he felt the smallness of humanity and, at the convent in Chartreuse, what he called 'an awful solitude' where he sensed the majesty of Nature speaking from an alpine throne: 'be this one spot of earth devoted to eternity!'

The moment of crossing the Alps was disappointing. He had expected something more momentous, 'the breathless wilderness of clouds', a peak experience, but the crossing was achieved without him even knowing and it took a passing peasant to tell him it had happened. There is something humbling in this story of a poet and a peasant, but despite the disappointment of the crossing Wordsworth kept faith with the power of imagination and the power of hope. One small human in the majestic vastness, it was not despair that filled him, but desire. Whatever vicissitudes one endures, the journeyman is always strangely expectant; Wordsworth's infinity was pregnant with hope. He wrote:

> Our destiny, our being's heart and home,
> Is with infinitude, and only there;
> With hope it is, hope that can never die,
> Effort, and expectation, and desire,
> And something evermore about to be.

> (*Prelude* Book VI, ll.604–8)

Brave and tenacious, this journey to the heart's home is a journey that one can be proud to make, but it is not a journey into pride.

Wordsworth's alpine crossing was, after all the energy expended and risks survived, a disappointment. It was humbling to be directed by a peasant and have his arrival announced after the fact. It was not at all what he had been led to expect. Stephen Petrus with his bandaged arm and his daily charnel house pilgrimage participates in humility. Looking at death every day, he is glad to live, and carries his pain a little more lightly. The human moment is brief, these stories say, and likely fraught with pain and disappointment, but it is beautiful. This I think is the essence of humility – not a grovelling negation of the self, but the grace to admit one's weakness and to receive enough love, strength or grace for each day. 'Are you on the path of true humility?' this charnel house is asking me. Humility? I don't even know if I have the courage to wish for this.

We can't all get to Naters, but we can find ways to open ourselves to the humble path. There are invitations to humility round about us all the time in the majesty of nature and in the presence of other people, and there are invitations that come from further afield. Ash Wednesday, for instance, is an annual open invitation to get in touch with reality. In churches all over the world people gather to be quiet, to reflect, to get into the queue with everyone else and be marked with ashes. You don't have to be signed up to faith to do this. You just join the human queue and accept, when the person at the front marks your forehead, that ordinary dust is your origin and your end. Something about the physical nature of this event – queuing, waiting, letting dirt be smeared on your skin, resisting the urge to rub it off – takes the idea of humility and makes it real. There is a liberating moment of truth when the poignant words wash over you: 'Remember oh woman, remember oh man, you are dust. And to dust you shall return.'

Humility by its very nature is a tricky thing; the moment you sense it with you it is gone. Dynamic rather than static, it visits like a breeze. You can only lean yourself in its direction by bringing yourself under a truth that is bigger than you are, and hope to be touched by it. There can be no humility certificate framed on your wall and no proof of purchase. We cannot acquire humility, or achieve it or earn it or gain it; but we might, if we are lucky, meet it one day on an ordinary path. It is like happiness, I think: another one of those butterflies that will not be caught or held, but lands on you when you are still.

6

Grave Statements

We think the story is linear – beginning, middle and end. But 'Once upon a time' is a phrase whose words curl, tail over nose, like a sleeping cat. The beginning is not precise and I wonder whether all our stories in fact, not just the fairytales, are like this: ropes of twisted time, weaving one beginning to the end of another. The old man dies as the lusty boy is born, as if the breath had passed from one to another in a great incomprehensible chain of being.

My father died in winter, on 26 December. He 'went home', as my mother said, for Christmas. Cancer of the liver – long, slow and inexorable. We had had years to prepare. Still the moment took us blind. I know why people use the phrase 'slipped away' for Death can steal you so silently. With my weary mother asleep in the hospice bed next to his, and my eldest brother curled up on a camp mattress at its foot, between the moment when my sister kissed his head and the moment she returned from the bathroom, he was gone.

We had watched my father by increments growing ever so slowly weaker, smaller; his flesh falling in tired tiers, without an appetite for its bones falling away into loose unanchored folds. His skin had become like fine paper, the bones beneath protruding and pronounced. Every bit of him ached, yet he still kept his zest for life, weakly waving a toy balloon when his youngest grandchild entered the room. He did not want to die.

That same December day was also, coincidentally, the day that the baby boy we were so longing to adopt was born. We had waited four years to be chosen. I had met several times with his birthmother, a small-boned, gutsy woman with wavy hair and freckles, who spoke with a southern twang and had hungry, hazel eyes. Despite being beset with addictions, she was a generous person, whose first son, whom she was parenting, was adorable; but she was struggling and she wanted something different for her second son. We had talked and confided, her eyes sometimes calm, sometimes darting disconcertingly between hollow and fiery as we made plans together for his future; and I had felt so privileged to be asked to be there with her for his arrival. The phone call saying that she had gone into labour came as I sat at my father's bedside taking my turn to bring the cup of water to his lips and adjust his pillows. He was breathing slowly and shallowly with long intervals between breaths; we knew it wouldn't be long, but the nurses thought there might be time enough to go to the birth and return. I so much wanted his last grandson to meet him before he died. So, with his family alongside him, I left my father's bedside just before midnight and rushed with my husband and daughter to a hospital two hours away to be at the birth of our son.

My husband entertained our four-year-old while I ran down the corridors to find our future son's birthmother, already in close contractions, frantic with fear and unattended by a midwife. Greatly relieved to be together, we fell into each other's arms, happy and anxious, clinging to one another the way survivors do in a crash. Thrown upon each other's charity, we were uninhibited by our disparities of education and life experience. We were totally, baldly human. Two women from opposite poles simply committed to the flourishing of this new person, we were determined for his happiness, sharing a single hope; and afraid. It was not a simple birth; there was much noise and some confusion and a nurse who spoke little English. There was the impossibility of an epidural. There was the late but welcome arrival of a larger-than-life, capable, African-American, female doctor who settled everything admirably, taking charge like a captain in a storm.

Josiah, as he is now named, came into the world in the early hours of the morning bursting with life, wailing as loudly as a train, with lusty lungs and a leaping erection. He couldn't have been more ready to live. His birthmother, his birth-grandmother, the social workers, my husband and I, all were elated to meet him. We all held and kissed him, we cried and laughed and blessed his beautiful beginning. We were full of joy. He was strong and he was very beautiful. He was loved. But it turned out that his birthfather was not the man whom everyone had thought, and Josiah would therefore grow up with skin darker than ours. Unacceptably darker, according to social services. He couldn't belong with us, they said. And we couldn't belong with him.

Reeling slightly as this news unfolded, I tried to adjust my future, and not just mine but his, and our family's and his birthmother's. The space we had made for him felt jagged as a wound, and all her hopes lay dashed. I swallowed the tears; there was a frightened and distraught birthmother, and a tiny baby with no home. This was not the time to examine my losses – these people needed to be held and loved. My husband, the birthmother and I passed Josiah back and forth, battling attachment; we three clutched each other's hands, choking even on the softest words. We knew that if there wasn't another family with acceptable skin waiting, he would go into care. Despite our brave intentions, our eyes began to leak and, in a circle of searing pain, we prayed that another family soon would be found for Josiah, so that he could go without delay to his new home and be loved as he deserved. A nurse who had heard only that we were not going to adopt came in and smiled at the baby, and then, as she looked up, her face contorted horribly. Her eyes pinched to a squint and poisonous words came spurting from her lips – how people like us should never be allowed near children, how racists were not wanted. Stunned by her hatred, speechless in a day in which words had already proven wholly inadequate, I turned to take a phone call from my sister.

In a ragged voice she said: 'I have bad news.'

So there, in one brutal day, two men were taken from my life: a father and a son, a past and a future. I remember the tears, great torrents of them, and the uncontrollable sobs that tore out of me. I did not know in the days that followed what I was crying for most, which loss was the most hateful one; I could not differentiate or prioritize anything to do with these losses. There was just one large angry bruise that seemed to take up the whole of my waking days. In such times the body, its needs and routines, are like a keel that keeps the boat from overturning; and it is a great blessing to have others who depend on you, whose needs require you to emerge, to speak the familiar and to retain a sense of courtesy and decorum.

Josiah went to live with a loving family who already had a biracial son, in a country that now has a biracial president. I put the small clothes I had sewn for him in a drawer. I never heard about him again.

My father, whose life left him as Josiah's emerged, was cremated and interred in the same grave as my grandfather, buried right on top of him, in the next layer up. Not, as one might have expected, in the grave of his own father, but in that of my mother's father – a man of proud principles whom he had never met. So why did he choose a different blood family from his own? Why did he want to belong there, in the grave with a stranger, in the windswept yard of a church in which he had never worshipped, in a state from which he had moved away some twenty years earlier? It wasn't as if he had hated his own father and mother, who had in fact bought a plot – what American mortuary jargon calls a 'pre-need memorial estate' – big enough for their whole family. There was a space waiting for him, next to his own kin, but he didn't take it.

These experiences left me with deep questions. In life and in death what is it that makes us belong and to whom? Do we choose belonging? Why could Josiah not belong with us? Why did my father belong with his father-in-law? Where would I belong one day?

* * *

Many of us wonder, if we think about it at all, where we belong. We live in an age of unprecedented global migration. I am the youngest of five children, and for generations our family lived locally. We came from Switzerland to America in 1763 on grounds of religious persecution, Mennonites settling in Pennsylvania, safe among the Amish, the Quakers, the Shakers; and we stayed there in the undulating farmland of Eastern Pennsylvania, never moving more than a county or two in two hundred years. Then, in the space of one generation we upped and moved: first, as a whole family, to the south; then three of five children went abroad, married Europeans, and dispersed. We are not unique. Our towns and cities, our neighbourhoods are now made up of persons from all over the world who have moved seeking political, social, religious, financial freedom, or simply seeking any kind of employment, or in some cases adventure. Some have moved believing the promise that you can be a new person in a new place. Or simply because they can, for international law allows more movement and modern transportation facilitates it. We are the most mobile generation ever to live on the face of the globe.

In East Kent, where my husband was born, there are villages named Hawkinge, Ruckinge and Sellinge, places that contain as a fragment our family name, Inge. And in the phone book there are clusters of Tipplers and Fullers, surnames that match the ones listed in the front of his old family Bible. When we visit family in Kent we walk from farm to cottage on footpaths over fields sown and harvested for generations by familial hands. We wander with our children through a churchyard where tilting stones mark the resting place of Mary Amanda Tippler and ivy-covered John Inge, my husband's great-grandparents, to the church in which my husband was christened; then back to lunch with cousins at an old mill house in which fifty years ago his christening party, photographed in black and white, took place and where, generations before, a dusty cousin who was a miller lived. If my husband belongs anywhere surely it is here. Wouldn't it be right for his bones one day to lie in the place where for generations people of his blood and bone have been lowered into the earth, and where his infant head was washed, water and earth embracing him under the same Kentish sky?

Or does he belong to the people of Worcester? He is their bishop after all, and his predecessors sleep beside their deans in the cathedral's cloister garden. Does giving your life to people mean they own you after death as well? After all, marriages have so claimed people since time began. Women, mostly, taken into the families of their men. But men too, like my father, are taken into the families of their wives. Does where you choose to spend your life mean more than where you come from? Do the people you choose become your family? And are these ties stronger than blood? For many people they seem to be.

Perhaps one's bones belong to a landscape. The English poet

John Betjeman's remains rest on the side of the churchyard of St Enodoc's in Cornwall, a church half-swallowed up in sand, uncertain whether it is emerging from the soil or sinking into it. He had enjoyed childhood holidays there and in his last years he lived nearby; it was a place he chose because, deep in his bones, he felt restored, renewed, revived by the Cornish coast. You can sit there next to his bones and breathe the air familiar to him and gaze out across the sloping fields to the river and the sea beyond, a water-shining, lustrous view still unmarred by intrusions. You can hear the same cry of gulls that he would have heard. Long after his eyes have become the food of worms you can open yours to claim the calm which that particular place promised him.

* * *

The deposition of human remains always makes a statement. In their last wills and testaments the dead speak unambiguously in the legal language of term and codicil, whereas in their choice of grave the dead speak in the language of symbol. Here people voice the unspoken or sometimes the unspeakable, often leaving their reasons unexplained – like my father, the disposal of whose remains raised as many questions as it answered. That doesn't offend me. In fact, there is an honesty about it that I admire. He didn't tell me everything about himself in life, and I don't expect to know him perfectly either in death. You can love without knowing entirely. Most of us do.

It is perhaps partly because many of us die with things left unsaid that the disposal of remains becomes a kind of final utterance. Your choice of a burial site is perhaps one of the last things you *can* say. And, if that place is marked and public, you go on saying it for as long as the stones survive. One of the best-known 'statement graves' of this sort in England is that of the English tenor, Peter Pears, and the composer, Benjamin Britten, in Aldeburgh. The pair lived as a couple in a time when it was infamy to do so, but they found in Aldeburgh a haven. Britten once wrote of his home on the Suffolk coast: 'I belong at home in Aldeburgh ... all the music I write comes from it.' Their burial side by side says, in a way that could not be articulated formally before their deaths, that they also belonged to each other.

Sometimes the last thing said is unintentional. I once came across a gravestone on the floor of an English country church where the deceased's family had run out of money to pay a stone carver who had charged them per letter. The name of the deceased was recorded, along with her dates. But when it came to the inscription which was meant to read 'Glory be to the Father, and to the Son, and to the Holy Ghost', there were simply the words 'Glory be to ye Father, & ye rest'. In perpetuity this stone confesses a love that exceeds its purse.

No less unintentional, though more serious, is the message that the English poet Philip Larkin took from the tomb of the 10th Earl and Countess of Arundel, whose effigies lie side by side in Chichester Cathedral. Originally companionable but discreet, these recumbent statues were altered upon restoration so that the Earl's hand, slipped from its gauntlet, is holding hers. There they lie, he in his armour, she in her aulic finery, and that part of him that is unclad casting in stone the most common of human bonds. 'What will survive of us is love', writes Larkin.

Instinctively I want this to be true. Indeed, I yearn for this to be true. And I know that I am not alone in this wish, for the same sentiment can be found in countless poems and books, and even in the picture books that I have read to my children. We humans cannot believe that this great energizing force, this lifespan of longings fulfilled and unfulfilled, expressed and unspoken, that we call love can simply cease. It seems too great a thing ever to be extinguished. That love survives, my whole heart leaps to say. And yet, it makes no sense, for love is an action as much as a feeling: when I stir for the fourth time in the middle of the night to go to my troubled child's bedside, I might be feeling intense frustration, but what I am doing is love. Love is active. Even were love merely a feeling, it would still require a living creature in order to exist, just as an action requires an actor.

What can we possibly mean when we say that what survives of us is love? Who is doing the loving and who is receiving it? If we say that the love lives on in those whom the deceased has loved, as if they had become saturated with love that would squeeze itself out in the world, this is no better. For the love that leaks from them onto the ones they in turn love is *their* love, not some imported love. We want our loves particular, not amorphous – the love of the beloved, not second-hand generic love. I do not wish it to be true but a part of me admits that, if we simply cease to be, our loving too must cease.

Unless of course we say that loving is a kind of energy which continues when the matter to which it is bound ceases. Or unless we hope for a resurrection.

*   *   *

We have lost so many of our stories. One of the most significant of these, I believe, is our loss of a narrative of meaning which for countless people over many generations was rooted in an overarching story of faith. In Philip Larkin's poem 'Church Going' he stands in a building that for many has lost its day-to-day impor-tance, imagining its eventual emptiness and how when it is a ruin it will still speak something its listeners can hardly understand. 'And what remains when disbelief has gone?' asks Larkin. The answer he gives is: a sense that here was held in unity 'what since is found only in separation'.

While Larkin's poem suggests that in the 'cross of ground' we understand ourselves and the transitions in our lives – marriage, baptism, death – in terms of what holds them and us together, increasingly we understand ourselves and our transitions in terms of collapse. We understand the parameters of marriage at its divorce rather than at its duration, and death as a finality rather than a gateway. Where a medieval worldview understood life by how it held together, we who have dissected the tadpole and divided the atom understand our world as much by how it falls apart. This is not a condemnation. This way of thinking has brought us so very many rewards, but it has also left us in some ways fragmented. Not only are we physically more mobile, we are also spiritually more eclectic, picking and mixing from a range of philosophies and beliefs. Added to this is a kind of social looseness – through social mobility and through social networking, we scatter our seeds of friendship more widely than ever before. We may belong less profoundly to any one place, but we visit a wider variety of places; we may not belong to any one person for a lifetime, but in the tabulation of virtual friends many belong to us.

Perhaps the increasing tendency to scatter ashes is one expression of these scattered lives. Apparently happy not to be remembered past the living memory of those family and friends who have loved us in life, we mingle with the earth in unmarked places, on hilltops, and at sea. Is this, I wonder, because we haven't stayed in one place long enough to feel that we belong there deeply? Does place no longer spell out belonging? Or is it simply that length and depth are not the same thing – that we may feel deeply drawn to places with which we have no lengthy connection.

It is not at all uncommon for our dying wishes to name a place for the scattering of ashes that is a place we loved but not one in which we lived – rather one that we visited, one that revived our souls, much as Betjeman's was revived by the Cornish coast. Here we were taken out of ourselves, or restored to ourselves. Here we felt most alive. This seems to me to be marking not where we lived our everyday lives but where we wish we'd lived. We must attempt a final arrival at some longed-for place. Is this an interpretation of heaven, I wonder? We have no idea where our soul may go, but we want to make sure our body ends up somewhere special. I can see the attraction of this, but I can't help also feeling that the implication of wanting to be scattered somewhere that meant something to us is that the ordinary neighbourhoods of our days had not enough meaning for us. It is as if we have spent a life wishing to be elsewhere, or focused on somewhere we are not. We have lost either the will or the ability to see that where we are is the place of meaning.

* * *

Once you start carrying a book around in your head everything seems to echo: articles you read, snippets you hear on the radio, poems, facts, scientific discoveries all clamour to fill its empty pages. In this rather unruly fashion I have acquired a whole array of fascinating accounts of the unusual places bodies can go when they die. Ashes can, for instance, be mixed with oil paints for a specially commissioned picture. Being largely carbon, they can be compressed with other carbon into a manufactured diamond. In Herefordshire two years ago one man had the ashes of his son mixed with ink and tattooed under his skin so that his son might 'be with him forever', as the newspaper said. This comforted the father, though the forever of a forearm would never be enough for me.

One very practical ending, and perhaps a fitting one for people who all their lives have loved to work, is to let their bodies work in death as medical cadavers dedicated to the advance of science. The thirteenth-century Arab scientist who discovered the explosive properties of potassium nitrate derived from wood ash would, I think, be fascinated by the modern twist that you can mix human ash remains into the saltpetre of fireworks. If faith cannot get you there, well, modern cocktails of potassium nitrate at least can ensure you are shot into sparkling heaven in the guts of a zinging rocket.

These are just a few of the extraordinary new ways we are dealing with human remains. Such innovations are a huge departure from any funereal practices ever recorded. They have in common a wish to do something either remarkable or enduring with our remains, and a feeling that what we have done in the past is not remarkable or enduring enough.

Alongside personal innovations of this sort come eco-experiments that aim to return something of value to the earth. *Eternal Reefs* near Atlanta, Georgia invites the families of the dead to bring their ashes, mix them with cement and pour them into large bell shapes which are then sunk at sea to create artificial reefs to supplement the natural reefs that are so swiftly deteriorating. Tokens from the dead (a medal, a watch, a memento), handprints, messages may be pressed like totems into the fresh cement, a brass name plaque is added, and there is a service of dedication at sea. Certificates are given to the families, who can also order silver pendants with the loved one's sea coordinates engraved on them or memorial plaques and t-shirts. If you have the means to do so, you can scuba dive on the anniversary of death to visit the fishy grave.

What intrigues me is that, although firmly physical, the whole project relies on a hope of eternity as one of its driving forces. It is implicit not only in the name of the firm but also in the stated intention of the founder, whose father wanted 'to be surrounded by life forever'. *Eternal Reefs* state that their reefs are made to last forever and that they are designed 'for people who are not done living'. There is a clear desire here to see death not as an end but as a continuation of life. Though of course the loved one's body is, in fact, utterly dead. Whatever is living down there is entirely marine.

Woodland burials, too, aim to combine the wish to go somewhere beautiful with the desire to carry on doing good or being active even in death. Although this is a fairly recent practice in the United States, it is slightly longer established in the UK – there are woodland burial sites in thirty counties in Britain. Religious or non-religious markers may be used, but on both sides of the Atlantic the single uniting feature of these new burial options, the thing that 'sells' them to an enquiring public, is an overarching concern for the environment – woodland burial avoids the mercury emissions and other pollutants of cremation. It does not require the consumption of fuel or create greenhouse gases, and it releases pressure on land by preserving rather than gobbling up wildlife habitats.

One of the first conservation burial sites in the United States is Ramsey Creek Preserve in the mountains of South Carolina. This thirty-three-acre site, which opened in 1998, protects a quarter-mile of the stream and its surrounds. A walk through the preserve takes you along the Ramsey Creek as it drops along five rock shoals, through mainly deciduous woodland some of which has never been ploughed. Within this constant sound of falling water, 220 species of native plants thrive in a habitat that includes a full range of wildlife from snaking water moccasins to treetop squirrels and even the occasional black bear. A love of nature is what the place was made for. The chapel's botanical windows feature violets, jack-in-the-pulpit, apple blossom, iris. On a table at the back are books about wildflowers and butterflies alongside offerings of pebbles and pine cones and an empty turtle carapace.

I visited Ramsey Creek with my family on a sunny day in mid-October. It was not hard to find. 'You turn right after the Mennonite swing-maker's house', said Dr Campbell, standing with his arms crossed, grinning in the sunlight, with sandy light-brown hair and freckles and a small gold hoop earring in his left ear that seemed incongruous above his blue medical tunic.

We had driven just over an hour out of Greenville, with two cranky children in the back seat. It was too beautiful a day to be stuck in a car on a faceless Wal-Mart and Burger King road while the not-so-distant mountains bloomed in autumn's best russet and gold. Adding to our frustration, the address we had in the town of Westminster took us not to the preserve at all but to a medical practice operating from a double-fronted former shop in an old-timey, brick-built strip with false façades and a covered walk in front. Main Street. It looked the brick equivalent of a Wild West town, without the swinging saloon doors. 'Closed for training day' scrawled on a bit of scrap paper was stuck in the window of the medical practice. I squinted and peered between the blinds. Nothing about the Ramsey Creek Preserve. And then I remembered that its founder was a doctor. Maybe this was the right address after all. Too bad it was the wrong day. I sighed. Then, just as we were about to head off, he appeared.

I got the feeling Billy Campbell was pleased to see us. Or maybe he was simply pleased with life. Easy to talk to, he nodded and smiled, happy in his skin. Sure, we could have our picnic in the preserve, he said, there were some tables down there, or we could just sit by the stream if we wanted. Disappointed that his English wife was not there to meet some people all the way from England, he told us about the small chapel they had moved to the preserve and the barn they had built, about the walking trails and the Mennonite farmers who were moving down from Ohio to settle in these fertile mountains.

The swing-maker's house was easy to spot. Neat and well-built, there were, standing in front of it, a selection of gazebos for sale and a porch full of wooden swings, single and double, just like the ones I had seen so many times on the porches of Plain Folk in my childhood. Glider chairs too, that rocked on side arms rather than on cumbersome runners. Smooth and fluid, no porch swing since has ever rocked like one of those. I could almost feel the summers of my grandma's porch. From beyond the screen door would come the clatter and chat of kitchen aunts, a smell of mint crushed in tawny tea, then the icy chink of cubes against my startled teeth.

Our October picnic at the preserve, however, was hurried by hunger. We sat in sawdust in a weathered wooden barn that was strung with fairylights and vines and filled with the satisfying scent of freshly-cut wood. Above, in a light and airy loft where double doors opened to mango-coloured treetops, we finished our melons in a tranche of warm sunlight. At home in this warm, drowsy American air, I would have liked to doze. But there was work to do – exploring.

We walked down trails that led into more trails, marked with little wooden signs, along a ridge for a while that fell sharply towards the sound of water. Here and there along the way on either side of the trail native stones would appear, lying flat, half-covered in woodland detritus, with words peeking out from the edge of curled-up leaves. Name only, or name and dates, or name and simple title: 'Husband', 'Sister', 'Together again'. Some leaf-covered stones revealed nothing more than themselves, others contained a message. Half-hidden by a clump of fern, not far from the pious 'With Jesus', lay the impish 'Later Babe'. Pushing leaves from one, my daughter discovered the postcard words 'Dear Nature, Thank you, Evelyn.'

Scampering from stone to stone uncovering words, scrabbling after chipmunks, we simply didn't notice the mounds at first.

Suddenly I realized what one was. I spotted several dotted near the trail, and then, as I looked for them, deeper in the woods many more at irregular intervals. Small mounds already growing ferns and cyclamen before the ground had settled. Some had dates. Nine years on, and still not smooth. I stopped and peered between the trees as far as I could see. The recent dead were all around us. I shivered.

If a battle from the Civil War had been fought in these woods, as well it might have been, the fallen might have lain just like that, scattered, randomly, where they fell. I felt a lot of things – the slight indelicacy of trespassing here on these recent griefs; the eagerness of earth to take us back; how much more pleasant it might be to end up here rather than in a treeless municipal cemetery mown weekly and fenced in by iron bars; the brevity of life. We walked on. More dates. Yet another youngish person. So many of them were young. One stone, half-upright on a partially sunken mound, read: 'I only know that/ Summer sang in/ me a little while/ that sings no more.' Glad of a bit of poetry, I paused. And then, my reverie was severed by the loud halloo of children finding something fun.

It was a hole. Perfectly rectangular, about four foot deep, cut clean and straight through six inches of brown topsoil and then Carolina clay. There were dark stones in the red clay walls and small white circles where cut roots gasped in the unfamiliar air, aghast at the abruptness of their injury. Alongside this hole a large mound of red soil lay on a spread tarpaulin. It looked so incongruous, that rectangle, the lines of it so sharp, the only straight lines anywhere to be seen. Its rigidity was entirely out of place – a barbarous regularity in an undulating, slightly chaotic landscape. And it was made: the only manufactured thing in acres of uninstructed nature. Made and left behind. This bold rectangle lay as if a discarded door had been tossed among the trees with blind impertinence by some dereliction crew.

With wild abandon, my younger child jumped into it. Standing up to her shoulders in that death-shaped pit she beamed up at me with delight. 'Look, mummy, a den!' she called. 'Come in!'

I demurred.

'Come on', she urged.

Startling as it was to see her in a grave, I did not yank her out. She was not in danger. The sides were not high. Either innocence or daring had hurled her there; she is rich in both, and they are qualities I admire and love in her. But I could not join her. That rectangle was a space too particular in purpose, and that purpose cruelly intimate; only innocence could enter such a space without violating it. A grief had started. Someone's someone, not so different from me or my husband, tall among the trees, or one of my urgent children, would lie there. And the red soil would cover them. I looked at the displaced mound of red soil set to one side and wondered how even that large a quantity could ever fill so great a hole, because the space she now was playing in seemed profoundly hungry, as if it could go on swallowing forever and not be filled. I never knew before that void could be a territory.

Her fingers ran with eager fascination over pebbles and roots, looking for interesting finds. As she picked stones from its smooth cut walls, clumps of earth fell to the clean floor, and I thought of a family's sorrow, and the habit we have of arranging things tidily in the face of death's chaos. We needed not to muss the preparations. They are a mark of respect. It was time.

'Come on,' I called, 'look, Daddy's way up the trail. Let's see if we can catch him.' I extended my hand. She didn't need it.

* * *

Only a state away from Ramsey Creek Preserve, near Atlanta, Georgia, Honey Creek Plantation also offers a natural burial service.

Honey Creek is much larger, on a site covering 2,000 acres of woodland, and when I discovered that it is based in the grounds of a Cistercian Monastery of the Holy Spirit I felt as though several small threads of this book strangely came together. Photos of the monks there showed me men in the same white habits with black scapula as would have been worn by the monks at Sedlec, centuries earlier and an ocean away.

Cistercians have always lived close to the earth; these modern Cistercians have taken it upon themselves to save 2,000 acres of wilderness. Committed to silence and solitude, they write: 'Some people have suggested that we sell bits and pieces of the land in order to take care of the Monastery well into the future. However we continue to believe that the property is not just for us but is a sacred trust that needs protecting for future generations, not only for monks, but for all those who hunger for places of peace, beauty and tranquillity.' As the city of Atlanta rapidly grows out to meet them, their land has become essential for providing that solitude and silence which are hallmarks of the Cistercian Order and into which they 'warmly invite all people'. I have always loved the woods and would be happy to end up in such a place myself although, if I could choose any woods in which to be buried, they would be either in the hills of North Carolina or in Pennsylvania, where the cocktail of hemlock and mountain laurel is blended to the perfect smell of home.

All of these woodland burial sites, whether English or American, aim to save, restore or establish significant wildlands. Burials must be 'dust to dust' with no embalming fluids, no vaults and only biodegradable caskets. One company I visited in England now makes woollen coffins. They come in the colours of sheep – creamy white or light brown with dark trims – and are lined with organic cotton.

Idealistic as these options may sound, they are mainly marketed in utilitarian terms – an opportunity to make ourselves useful in death, as do those who devote their bodies to medical science. We are invited to give something back. But these green endings are not only utilitarian. For many people there is something verging on the spiritual about them. When the British naturalist Professor David Bellamy, an enthusiastic supporter of woodland burial, writes, 'I can think of no better way of celebrating the continuity of creation than becoming part of a tree in a piece of countryside destined to become woodland, full of wild flowers, wildlife and birdsong, for ever and ever, Amen', there is the ring of a prayer about his words.

I would not want to belittle the spiritual value of woodland burial any more than the spiritual value of any other kind of burial. But it is easy to muddle utility, spirituality and the expiation of guilt in one unthought bundle. Green burials plug into our modern Western guilt about having used too much of the world's resources in our lives. In our death we are given the chance to make amends by becoming food for trees, by our purchase of a green burial site helping to contribute to the preservation of a parcel of wild land, by the planting of trees on a new woodland site increasing the contribution of oxygen to the planet, or by restoring marine habitat. All have in common a deep attachment to the physical world. This world is the one to which we are making a final contribution. When that decision is the culmination of a life governed by environmental issues it seems a fitting end; when it is a kind of attempt to pay back the earth for a life spent abusing it, it is not so very dissimilar from a medieval indulgence: live however you like and then buy this piece of land to ensure a beneficent end. In this way our green salvation is less an expression of spirituality and more like our final consumer choice.

That so many choices exist is itself typical of Western modernity, but I believe there are further ways in which emerging trends in dealing with the dead mirror our times. Having lost a place we call home, we cast our remains to the wind. Less sure than we used to be about the existence of heaven, we create material paradises. Uncertain that we will live forever, but still longing to do so, we try to live on in marine reefs and preserved wilderness. Our loss of religious certainty, our loss of place and our longing for the eternal are all reflected in the increasingly inventive means of disposing of our bones. I suspect that beneath these displacements lie larger questions. Is there ultimate meaning at all? What is the story of our universe? Is it all a series of accidents?

Perhaps we do not know where our remains should belong because we do not know where we belong in this larger story. In fact, what we do know about our biological past and about the far reaches of space suggests that our brief lives have little meaning at all. We have relied so much on science to answer the big questions about where we come from and where we are going, and it has told us this: that we are blips in an ancient and unimaginably vast universe. This fills many with as much fear as the notion of eternal torment filled our ancestors.

In his classic philosophical and psychological study *The Courage to Be*, the twentieth-century German-American theologian and existential philosopher Paul Tillich describes the three stages of anxiety in the history of Western civilization: in the Ancient world, anxiety about our fate; in the Medieval world, an anxiety concerning guilt and condemnation; and in the Modern age, our anxiety about meaninglessness. In each age anxiety focused mainly, although not exclusively, on a particular concern.

Part of being human, Tillich argues, is anxiety, which will surface in different forms and become a fear. It seems to me that the fear it becomes depends on the story in which we understand ourselves as living. In an age of fate, the fear is that the story is already written, that we are merely passive players. In an age of judgement, the fear is that the part we play is doomed, that our actions and intentions are never good enough. In an age of meaninglessness, the fear is that there is, in the end, no story.

Where the ancient Age of Fate may have offered the possibility of nobility through resignation, and the medieval Age of Judgement bred a sense of the possibility of justice, the Age of Meaninglessness seems devoid of classical virtues, for these develop within a narrative and meaninglessness by its nature undermines plot. So perhaps the gift of an Age of Meaninglessness is that one may feel freer to look in various directions.

Mainly we look for meaning backwards – 'where have we come from?' is the great Darwinian question that has dominated our investigative urges in recent times. Not at all confident about where we are headed as a human race, we do however feel fairly confident about the direction from which we have come. Our questions of origin are being answered in new ways all the time and, although there are still large and significant gaps in our knowledge, we understand more than we ever have before about how it all works: our bodies, our minds, our planet, our universe. But the 'why?' question remains.

In fact the 'why' question seems to have grown larger and more pressing as our attention has been focused on finding the answer to 'how'. Look at all the anxiety we now have about happiness, about wellbeing, about the meaning of life. The self-help industry and the wellbeing gurus all try to address this nagging question of why – what is it all about, what does it all mean? What fascinates me is that, in this dramatic cultural and psychological change from the medieval to the modern, bones have remained a primary carrier of our hopes and fears. Where the medieval mind took particular care of human remains in the fear of eternal judgement, the modern mind looks for solutions that combat the fear of ultimate meaninglessness. The questions may be different, but the carrier of those questions is largely unchanged: robust and fragile, renewing and inescapable, our bodies, and in particular their most enduring elements – our bones.

* * *

During my travels bones have become for me a metaphor for the enduring and essential, the deep things that remain once all the skin and the muscle of life is gone. There they lay, hard core of our soft bodies, perhaps one of the firmest things in our fluid lives. On a planet that is mostly water we are people made mostly of water with this one rigid element – our bones. Two hundred and six of them. Around this remarkable, renewable frame cling every muscle, every sinew, every artery, every nerve, and in the protection of these bones hide our most vulnerable organs. Where some creatures wear their skeletons on the outside to protect their flesh, we come into life unarmoured, ready to be wounded. In fact, the first sign of independent life is the severed flesh of an umbilical cord.

Amazingly resilient as it is, our exterior is subject to an enormous degree of change. Yet, most of how we identify ourselves – our face, skin, hair, eyes – is carried on the outside. We primp and preen, we clothe and style, and we surgically enhance; and all the while our bones quietly carry us. The journey into bones is a journey into this interior. Not just, of course, the chemical and physical interior of calcium and cartilage, of red and yellow marrow, but a journey into the core of the body that corresponds with a journey into the centre of the self – that thing we sense when we say 'I feel it in my bones'. The bones are the firm frame of your body, this journey suggests – what is the central core of your self? Call it a soul if you will, whatever name you give it will not explain it entirely. The deep part; the thing that remains as flesh falls away.

Four charnel houses, it seems to me, have asked four disquieting questions: Are the broken parts of your deep self being healed? (Czermna.) Have you found a lasting hope? (Sedlec.) What are the things for which you will be remembered? (Hallstatt.) Are you on a path of true humility? (Naters.)

I want to live with those four questions and to try to answer them. Perhaps answer is not the right word. What I really mean is that I want to hold myself in some way answerable to them. Some questions I think remake us. Because they probe the corners of our psyche, because they do not go away. They work away at us and we work away at them and sometimes we carry them for a lifetime and yet the answer we come up with is not one that can ever be written down. When we finally go to say the words, we find – perhaps to our dismay – that they have already been spoken, not with our lips but with our lives.

* * *

There's something about bones. It's strange. We would not hesitate to discard a toenail, a tooth, a sweeping of hair. The skin of the dead is repulsive. But for bones we have a different regard. They are calcium just the same as a tooth or a toenail; just the same, they are dead. Their service is obsolete, they are bound to disintegrate. And yet, around the globe, over millennia and across cultural and religious divides human bones speak a language of common respect. I think I understand now at least part of why that is. I think it is because these bones are not merely the remains of a particular person; they are carriers of our common humanity, and bearers of shared hopes and fears.

In this book I have written about several kinds of fear. The fears I have experienced in childhood; in travelling; the fear of judgement that so characterized the medieval mind; the fear of meaning-lessness that besets us in the present day; and the fear of death, in which so many of these others meet. But there is another kind of fear that I have only recently begun to appreciate. It is a fear that has little to do with terror and more to do with awe and respect. It is what terror may become when its object is demystified – terror transformed, if you like.

When I return from my travels and stand at the mouth of my charnel house, this transformed fear is what I feel. Not frightened of the bones, but respectful of them. I respect them partly because of the simple fact that they are human. Like Vaclav Tomaszek, I want to credit value to the bones in my charnel house because they were people. That is reason enough. Because they lived and loved and suffered and joyed and died. And this last fact is also a particular reason why I respect them. However young or old, however rich or poor, they have done the dreaded thing. They have been where each of us fears and none of us has gone.

I respect them too because I am one of them, inheritor of their DNA, a sharer of their very matter. Their dust is my skin, renewing itself, along with my bones and every cell in my body, every seven years. Dust to dust I already am, and in this respect in death I shall only do what I have always done: change matter into matter.

For all of these reasons the fear I feel on my return is a different kind of fear. It is something similar to what I remember hearing described in my childhood as 'the fear of the Lord', which was not meant to be a terror or a dread, but a deep awe of and respect for God. The fear of my charnel house neighbours is something like that for me now. The bones do not frighten me, but I hold them in wonder and reverence. Both the fear and the reverence are saying that there is something big and not wholly understood here, something outside myself that connects with my deepest self in ways I cannot explain. It is akin to the Holy.

* * *

Thoreau went to the woods to live deliberately, to suck at the marrow of life, to look at bare essential things. I went to Silesia and back to stay with the sight of bare bones until they frightened me no more. Each stop on the way asked its questions of me, in bold and implacable silence. Thousands and thousands of eyeless sockets have stared me through, and sometimes in the face of those stares I felt as hollowed out as the honeycombed centre of a femur, light and febrile, easily snapped. 'What you are we were', they say with chilling calm, stacked chin on cranium in a tall wall of certainty, 'What we are you shall be'. And it is true. We are dust and to dust we shall return. This fills me with great sorrow, for I too want my small moment to be magnificent. But it fills me also with humility, and gratitude; and gratitude makes whatever we have enough.

I do not know how much more time I have to live my questions out, but I am glad I started asking them even before the cancer came for, although they cannot be rushed, these are questions that must not be avoided. This is true whether or not you have been diagnosed with a frightening disease. The questions these charnel houses asked of me stir me to life-enriching responses. *Are the broken parts of your deep self being healed?* Get rid of the bitternesses. Mend the bridges. Seek and receive forgiveness. Let yourself be loved. *Have you found a lasting hope?* Anchor yourself in the eternal and abiding (for me this is God). Feed yourself something stronger than optimism. You are in a constant state of growth and transition, so let change transform you. *What are the things for which you will be remembered?* Cut the crap in your life. Do the things that matter. Find and exercise your gifts. *Are you on a path of true humility?*

Submit to a truth that is bigger than yourself. Become part of it. Let it be your story. What I have been surprised to discover, as these questions chase and wash over me, is that preparing to live and preparing to die are in the end the same thing.

* * *

I have long been seduced by fear and by freedom, sensing that the two things are related, and liking them both for the taste they put in your mouth. Electric, tinged metallic. Take the coin of Thrill and toss it in the air. Its two faces whirl and blur – fear, freedom, fear, freedom – and then it lands. And the landing for me was always a disappointment. Even when you won, you lost something. You lost the blur. In the solid slap of palm upon the coin, whatever its upturned face, you lost the whirl.

Since this adventure began, another coin has been tossed into the air. It whirls past my ear like a whisper. I can almost see the blur of its two faces: death, life, death, life. Whichever way it lands I know the feeling will be freedom. Because freedom is inside me. It doesn't depend on the coin.

My story is a human story and a sacred story that joins with all such eternal stories from the chick-in-egg skeletons of Hallstatt's Neolithic necropolis to the woodland burials at Honey Creek Preserve. It is amazed at the things it sees, it ponders things it cannot see, it lives in love and hope. None of us can know whether the story we live by is provably true, only whether we are true to it. And that, I think, cannot be decided in a day. You see, here I am again, talking about life and how to live it well. Well, there are so many things I do not know. But one thing I hold close: living isn't something outside you that you will do one day when you have organized your life a little better. It comes from deep in the centre of yourself. You have to let the life in, there at the deepest part, and live it from the inside out. My visits to four charnel houses all say the same thing to me: Return. In your cellar is the salt of life.

* * *

Dark in a February evening I resolved to return to my own charnel house. The ink-black sky outside my tall study windows was speckled with orange city lights. Headlamp twins of homeward cars winked across the river bridge, and lights from under its stone arches smeared the swollen Severn below with yellow rippling stripes. The children were in bed. This time it was not so much that I didn't want them to know as that I didn't want to be disturbed. I wanted to take time with my cellar bones and listen to whatever they might murmur. And yet I had to wait, for I needed help lifting the trap door lid and my husband was reading our little one a story.

I listened with tingling ears to the undulations of his engaging voice but could not decipher the words. Deep rumblings which I took to be bears were followed by the high 'beep, beep' of some alerted vehicle. A discernible 'Oh no!' was followed by a murmur of narration. One delighted giggle chased a lusty laugh and the sweet childish voice I love so well demanded more. I love that little voice. And I am losing it. Every time I phone when I am away, to say goodnight or what time my train will arrive, I hear that it has altered incrementally since the last time I heard it over a telephone line, and I know that one day before too long I will phone up to find that the last bit of little child will have gone from it for ever.

So I listened, at my desk, with inky blackness pressing in at every pane. I listened with a kind of lover's hunger and I tried to imagine ways of describing it, so that I could hold it or, failing that, so that after it was gone I could summon it. If it were a colour, what colour would it be? If it were an animal, what animal would it be? If it were a song … and then, as if she had read my mind, she was singing, with her head on her pillow and it was not the nursery rhyme we sang a month ago, but a crooning song about a heartbeat. For already she was in love with a boy with curly hair and mischievous eyes and, before her baby voice had entirely left her, she was inviting her girl voice to come. The beauty and brevity of this life swelled in my solar plexus like a warm loaf of heavy bread.

But at last she slept, and we followed the twisting staircase down and down again, past the curious storerooms, cold and colder, their dark recesses flashed with bright ends of tricycle chrome and glinting jars of jam, through a crooked doorway where you had to duck a little, towards the charnel house. While my husband fiddled expertly with a screwdriver and the tricky lid, I struck the match and lit the black wick of our dinner candle stub. The short silver candlestick was smooth and cold between my fingers and thumb. The cover off, I stood at the mouth of the entrance pit, hesitating like a beginner at the edge of a diving board.

'Ooh, a bit spooky', I said over my shoulder with feigned lightness, peering down, then standing up again. He offered to go down first. 'No, I want to do it', I replied. It was half of the truth. I had not rid myself of reservations about death. I was neither sanguine nor careless in the face of this darkness.

I lower myself cautiously into the entrance pit. Ducking my head through the breezeblock gap I hold my candle up towards the medieval walls beyond, noticing as I didn't the first time the neatness of the stone work. Cut red sandstones, the same as those used in the cathedral, rise to a neat arch above, but there will not be space enough to stand unless I actually enter the chamber. Pressing further in, I hold the candle down towards my ankles.

There is a small gap or gulley that I must cross between the new breezeblock wall and the medieval one; about two feet wide and maybe three feet deep, it is not difficult but I want to find sure footing.

I see I was wrong the first time I came down here about there being nowhere to step. In fact, as I put my candle down around my feet, I see that there is a kind of path rising abruptly from just the other side of the gulley. Narrow as a sheep trail, it has been worn over and between rising mounds of bones. There are bones, not floor, beneath it, and at the edge, where the modern opening in which I am crouched has been cut, bits of bone jut out from below the path like the jagged struts of a broken basket.

I cannot work out what the path is made of. It looks like sandy concrete, but this makes no sense, and it is febrile and crumbly. Compacted dust perhaps? A trail of ashes? Hundreds of years of crushed skulls. I dread stepping across the gap onto what might prove to be crumbling dust, and the sound of cracking bone beneath my feet. I don't know how far down the stone floor is beneath these bones, how far I might fall were they to give way beneath me, and for one fearful moment I imagine myself suffocating under a tumble of skeletons. I pause.

As I stretch my candle arm, a cold chill of air steals up my sleeve, but I can see. Clearly others have walked here before me and I must trust their precedence. Crouching and stepping over the sharp shard of a splintered rib and avoiding the smooth crown of a skull, I cross the gap gingerly, first one foot, then the other. And then, with sure feet, I am inside, standing to full height, surrounded by heaped skeletons.

The candlelight, completely local, requires me to bring it and myself close to anything I hope to see and, as I stoop and rise, alternating clean sweeps of arch above and sloping mounds of bone below appear from and disappear back into darkness. In this candlelight I can see either what lies ahead of me or what lies beneath my feet, but I cannot see both at once. I must make this choice with every step. And so I go very slowly, raising the candle out in front, above, and then stooping down to illuminate my feet where femur-ends like fists thrust up between skulls, and yellowed teeth gleam in the upside-down hollow of a battered cranium.

Hot wax drips from its sideways tilt as the candle flickers. Swiftly I right it. I have left the matches on the table in the room behind me and if this candle goes out I will be in utter darkness. A dark grey femur juts out by my ankle, and rising I make a mental note not to trip. I press on, raising and lowering my small light, trying to discern the dimensions of this chamber. I am amazed how little light one candle gives and also how it changes everything. Being here without it is unthinkable.

I follow the compacted path slowly, tentatively, stopping to shine the light to right and left, above my head and down towards my feet. I want to see if that shape I sense before me is an ancient window or a door, and as I speak into the darkness I see my breath before me rise with every word in little clouds. I love that breath. I love that it is mine, alive down here in this cold charnel house, silvery like a spirit.

I raise the candle up, and find there is still room to stand, and only about twelve feet until the end. And then in tiny steps I am there, at the former entrance high up in the wall, once entered from the cathedral side, blocked up and hung with cobwebs so thick and long and so sullied by a hundred years of dirt that they look like blackened twine. They do not sway. There is no movement in the air, no breath but mine. Around me either side of this compacted path the mounds of skulls and bones in jumbled heaps lie still – cranial curves and the knuckle-ends of thighs, a skull-less mandible the bottom half of a macabre laugh. I am not afraid; but neither do I want to let the candle linger on that laugh. Heart thumping, I shine the light along the walls to illuminate, insofar as I can, the fanning arches of the vaulted ceiling, and see that I have reached the limit of this subterranean box.

With a strange reluctance I do not fully understand, I turn. Picking my way slowly along the route I came, I trust now the load-bearing capability of the path. I know where to avoid the tripping femur, and I anticipate the angle of the slope. There is no rush. I look at the candle stub burning low against the silver. How white the silver gleams. I love its perfect smoothness to my touch. A drip of wax spills over, lava to my startled finger. This too I love, this being alive with skin that burns. The rectangle of yellow light ahead shines into the entrance pit beyond me.

At the two-foot gap I pause. Of course I do not want to stay down here. And yet I hesitate; I am not likely to visit these bones again. It is not so much that I want to stay in this place as that I want its pace to stay with me. I like being able only to see what is ahead of me or what is at my feet but not both at once. I like having to pay attention. I want to thank the bones; they have taught me this. Not just here, but in Czermna and Sedlec, in Hallstatt and Naters.

To be present in a moment is not hard. But it takes all of you. You have to listen well and look long. You have to engage your heart, bringing your fear and your hope to the same place, for what is hope without an element of dread? Unless it teeters at the edge of loss it is a saccharine thing, a Disney wish. Unless it is prepared to set belief to work it is mere optimism. There is a bond between the living and the dead that is a kind of door to hope. We look at them and know what we shall be, and determine to do with our brief span some life-bringing thing. This is hope. Not waiting for a rescue, or to be woken from a sleep; not gambling on a bit of luck, not dreaming dreams, but bringing breath and love and sweat to bear upon the darkness.

As I clamber out, my husband hoists me up in one smooth stretch. With few, inconsequential words we replace the charnel lid, the panel of floor and its edging, the rug, the barley twist table and the chairs. I blow the candle out and pick the hardened wax. Upstairs, in almost monastic silence, we wash our dusty hands.

My study windows still are inky-black. I toss another log upon a dwindling fire, watching orange sparks that fly from it brief and bright, expiring in the moment that they thrive. They say it will be three degrees below zero tonight, and I am grateful for this heat as I am for the fire's promise of company. I am grateful for the basket full of logs, for the one who carried them here, for the one who chopped them, for the tree that grew a hundred years and died to make such heat.

I want to tell the bones what they have given me, but they have no ears to hear and no eyes to see. So I will tell it whole to those who still have flesh on, speaking from my bones to theirs while there is breath to do so and life to live the words out. The beautiful brevity of this life throbs in me like an overgrown heartbeat. It sings in my bones, it lifts my ribs as I stretch high to draw the curtains closed against the night. Till dawn I write.

Sources and Further Reading

Chapter 1: The Charnel House

Carrol, Rory, 'How Otzi the Iceman was stabbed in the back and lost his fight for life', *The Guardian*, 21 March 2002.

Chen, Dr Pauline, *Final Exam: A Surgeon's Reflections on Mortality*, London: Souvenir Press, 2008.

Heiss, A. G. and Oeggle, K., 'The plant macro-remains from the Iceman site (Tisenjoch, Italian-Austrian border, Eastern Alps): new results on the glacier mummy's environment', *Veget Hist Archaeobot* 18:23, doi:10.1007/s00334-007-0140-8.

Holden, T. G. 'The Food Remains from the Colon of the Tyrolean Ice Man', in Keith Dobney and Terry O'Conner, *Bones and the Man: Studies in Honour of Don Brothwell*, Oxford: Oxbrow Books, 2002, pp. 35–40.

Ives, Sarah, 'Was ancient alpine "Iceman" killed in battle?', *National Geographic News*, 30 October 2003.

Jha, Alok, 'Iceman bled to death, scientists say', *The Guardian*, 7 June 2007.

Pain, Stephanie, 'Arrow points to foul play in ancient iceman's death', *New Scientist Tech*, http://technology.newscientist.com/article/dn1080

Plato, *The Symposium*, trans. Walter Hamilton, London: Penguin Classics, 1951.

Rollo, Franco et al., 'Otzi's last meals: DNA analysis of the intestinal content of the Neolithic glacier mummy from the Alps', *Proceedings of the National Academy of Sciences*, 99 (20): 12594–9 (2002).

Thoreau, Henry David, *Walden*, intro. Bill McKibben, Boston: Beacon Press, 1997.

Waldron, Tony, 'The Human Remains from the Chapter House, Worcester Cathedral', *Archaeology at Worcester Cathedral: Report of the Twentieth Annual Symposium*, ed. Christopher Guy, Leicester: University of Leicester Press, 2011.
—*Paleopathology*, Cambridge: Cambridge University Press, 2008.

Chapter 2: Czermna

Bach, Aloys, *Urkundliche Kirchen-Geschichte der Grafshaft Glatz*, Breslau: 1841, 509.

Balfour, Henry, 'Life history of an Aghori Fakir; with an exhibition of the human skull used by him as a drinking vessel, and notes on the similar use of skulls by other races', *The Journal of the Anthropological Institute of Great Britain and Ireland*, vol. 26: 340–57.

Bello, Silvia, Parfitt, Simon and Stringer, Chris, 'Earliest Directly-Dated Human Skull-Cups', *PloS ONE* 6(2): e17026. doi:10.1371/journal.pone.0017026, 2011.

Benard, Elisabeth Anne, *Chinnamasta: The Aweful Buddhist and Hindu Tantric Goddess*, Delhi: Motilal Barnarsidass, 1994.

Browning, Reed, *The War of the Austrian Succession*, New York: St Martin's Press, 1993.

Cherry, Stephen, *Barefoot Disciple: Walking the Way of Passionate Humility*, London: Continuum, 2011.

Hastrup, Kirstin, *A Passage to Anthropology: Between Experience and Theory*, London: Routledge, 1995.

Kester Brewin, *Other: Loving Self, God and Neighbour in a World of Fracture*, London: Hodder and Stoughton, 2010.

Koudounaris, Paul, *The Empire of Death*, London: Thames and Hudson, 2011, pp. 95–6.

Kuwata, Tadachika, *Shincho koki (Chronicle of Nobunago)*, Tokyo: Shinjinbutsu, 1997.

Mader, W., 'Die Schädelkapelle von Tscherbeney', *Die Grafschaft Glatz: Zeitschrift des Glatzer Gebirgvereins* 4 (July–August, 1908): 1–2.

McArthur, M., *Reading Buddhist Art: An Illustrated Guide to Buddhist Signs and Symbols*, London: Thames and Hudson, 2004.

Medwin, Thomas, *Conversations of Lord Byron: Noted During a Residence with his Lordship* (1824), 70.

Traherne, Thomas, 'The Salutation', in *Thomas Traherne Poetry and Prose*, ed. Denise Inge, London: SPCK, 2002.

The Russian Primary Chronicle, a history of Kievan Rus 850–1110, trans. in English as *The Tale of Bygone Years*.

For images of Barbara's Bed and Breakfast visit: Chata Rysiowka. http://www.rysiowka.pl/contact.php

Chapter 3: Sedlec

Barry, Patrick, O.S.B., *St. Benedict's Rule: A New Translation for Today*, Hidden Spring, 2004.

Chadwick, Henry, 'Origen, Celsus, and the resurrection of the body', *Harvard Theological Review* 41 (1948): 83–102.

De Waal, Esther, *A Life-Giving Way: A Commentary on the Rule of St. Benedict*, Collegeville, MN: Liturgical Press, 1981.

Evans, Gillian R., *Bernard of Clairvaux (Great Medieval Thinkers)*, Oxford: Oxford University Press, 2000.

Fudge, Thomas, *Crusade Against Heretics in Bohemia, 1418–1437: Sources and Documents*, Surrey: Ashgate, 2002.

Gregory of Nyssa, *On the Soul and Resurrection*, trans. Catharine P. Roth, New York: St Vladimir's Press, 1993.

Hildegardis Scivias, trans. Columba Hart and Jane Bishop, New York: Paulist Press, 1990.

Kaminsky, Howard, *A History of the Hussite Revolution*. Berkeley: University of California Press, 1967.

Murphy, Nancy, *Bodies and Souls, or Spirited Bodies?*, Cambridge: Cambridge University Press, 2006.

Newman, Barbara J., *Sister of Wisdom: St Hildegard's Theology of the Feminine*, Berkeley: University of California Press, 1987.

Polkinghorne, John, *Exploring Reality*, New Haven: Yale University Press, 2005.

Ruether, Rosemary, 'Mothers of the Church: Ascetic Women in the Late Patristic Age', in Rosemary Ruether and Eleanor McLaughlin (eds), *Women of Spirit: Female Leadership in the Jewish and Christian Traditions*, New York: Simon and Schuster, 1979.

Walker Bynum, Caroline, *The Resurrection of the Body in Western Christianity, 200–1336*, New York: Columbia University Press, 1995.

Wright, N. T., *The Resurrection of the Son of God*, Minneapolis: Fortress Press, 2003.

Chapter 4: Hallstatt

Bandel, Klaus, 'Composition and ontongeny of Dictyoconites (aulacocerida, cephalopoda)', *Paläontologische Zeitschrift*, vol. 59, nos 3–4, 223–44, doI: 10.1007/BF02988810.

Barth, Fritz E., 'Archaeological heritage of the Hallstatt region', Foregs '99 Dachstein-Hallstatt-Salzkammergut Region, 83–9 (part of the Austrian application to the World Heritage Committee UNESCO).

Geramb, Marie Joseph, *Pilgrimage to Jerusalem and Mount Sinai, volume 2 (1840),* Whitefish, MT: Kessinger Publishing, 2009.

Jonnes, Jill, *Eiffel's Tower: And the World's Fair Where Buffalo Bill Beguiled Paris, the Artists Quarreled, and Thomas Edison Became a Count,* New York: Viking Adult, 2009, 163–4.

Koudounaris, Paul, *The Empire of Death: A Cultural History of Ossuaries and Charnel Houses,* London: Thames and Hudson, 2011.

Lobitzer, Harald and Mandl, Gerhard, 'A Brief History of Geological Research of the Dachstein-Hallstatt-Salzkammergut Region', Berichte der Geologischen Bundesanstalt, 2008.

Proust, Marcel, *In Search of Lost Time,* London: Vintage Classics, 1996.

Rebay-Salisbury, K., 'Cremations: Fragmented Bodies in the Bronze and Iron Ages', in K. Rebay-Salisbury, M. L. S. Sørensen and J. Hughes (eds), *Body Parts and Bodies Whole: Changing Relations and Meanings,* Oxford: Oxbow, 2010, pp. 64–71.

Rohn, J., Ehret, D., Moser, M. and Czurda, K., 'Prehistoric and recent mass movements of the World Cultural Heritage Site Hallstatt, Austria', *Environmental Geology,* vol. 47:5, 702–14.

Sjovold, Torstein, 'Testing Assumptions for Skeletal Studies by Means of Identified Skulls from Hallstatt, Austria', in *Grave Reflections: Portraying the Past through Cemetery Studies,* Shelly Saunders and Ann Herring (eds), Toronto: Canadian Scholars Press, 1995.

Trafton, Scott Driskell, *Egypt Land: Race and Nineteenth-Century American Egyptomania,* New Americanists, Durham, NC: Duke University Press, 2004.

Trigger, Bruce G., *A History of Archaeological Thought*, Cambridge: Cambridge University Press, 2007.

Whitehouse, Helen, Review Article: 'Egyptomanias', in *American Journal of Archaeology*, vol. 101, no. 1, January 1997, 158–61.

Other related articles:
'Austrian UNESCO World Heritage village outraged at plans for Chinese copy', *The Daily Telegraph*, 17 June 2011.

'Hallstatt – A Stairway to the Bronze and Iron Ages', *Athena Review* (Recent Finds in Archaeology), vol. 4, no. 2, 12–13.

Chapter 5: Naters

Addison, Joseph, *Remarks on Several Parts of Italy in the Years 1701, 1702, 1703*. T. Walker, 1773. Ch. 'Geneva and the Lake'.

Appleyard, Brian, *How to Live Forever or Die Trying: On the New Immortality*, London: Simon and Schuster, 2007.

Black, Ralph W., 'From Concord Out: Henry Thoreau and the Natural Sublime', *Interdisciplinary Studies in Literature and the Environment*, Oxford, 1994, 2(1): 65–76.

Burke, Edmund, *A Philosophical Enquiry into the Origin of Our Ideas of the Sublime and Beautiful* (1757).

Burnet, Thomas, *The Sacred Theory of the Earth*, London, 1684.

Cherry, Stephen, *Barefoot Disciple: Walking the Way of Passionate Humility*, London: Continuum, 2011.

Comte-Sponville, André, *Small Treatise on the Great Virtues*, London: Vintage, 2003.

de Beer, E. S. (ed.), *Diary of John Evelyn*, Oxford: Oxford University Press, 1955.

Gray, John, *The Immortalization Commission: Science and the Strange Quest to Cheat Death*, London: Allen Lane, 2011.

Gray, Thomas, *Works*, ed. Edmund Gosse, New York, 1885.

Harrington, Alan, *The Immortalist: An Approach to the Engineering of Man's Divinity*, St Albans: Panther, 1973.

Howell, James, *Epistolae Ho-Elianae: The Familiar Letters*, London, 1890.

Kant, Immanuel, *Observations on the Feeling of the Beautiful and Sublime*, trans. John Goldthwaite, Berkeley: University of California Press, 2003.
—*Critique of Judgment* (1790).

Koudounaris, Paul, *The Empire of Death: A Cultural History of Ossuaries and Charnel Houses*, London: Thames and Hudson, 2011.

Kurzweil, Ray, *The Singularity Is Near: When Humans Transcend Biology*, New York: Viking, 2005.

Kurzweil, Ray and Grossman, Terry, MD, *Transcend: Nine Steps to Living Well Forever*, New York: Rodale Books, 2009.

Mitford, Jessica, *The American Way of Death Revisited*, New York: Virago Press, 1998.

Moellering, Kurt, *William Wordsworth, Henry David Thoreau and the Construction of the Green Atlantic World*, PhD thesis, Northeastern University, Boston, MA, April 2010.

Murdoch, Iris, *The Sovereignty of Good*, London: Routledge, 1970.

Nicolson, Marjorie Hope, 'Sublime in External Nature', *Dictionary of the History of Ideas*, New York, 1974.
—*Mountain Gloom and Mountain Glory: The Development of the Aesthetics of the Infinite*, Ithaca, NY: Cornell University, 1959, reprint Weyerhaeuser Environmental Classics, 1997.

Nietzsche, Friedrich, *Human, All Too Human*, London: Penguin, 1994.

Price, Uvedale, *Essay on the Picturesque, As Compared With The Sublime and The Beautiful* (1794).

Ruskin, John, 'Of the Novelty of Landscape', *Modern Painters*, New York, 1856.

Thoreau, Henry David, *Walden*, intro. Bill McKibben, Boston: Beacon Press, 2004.

Wordsworth, William, *The Prelude*, 1850.
—*Guide to the Lakes*, London, 1906.

Chapter 6: Grave Statements

Bede, *Ecclesiastical History of the English People*, iv, 19–20.

Bray, Alan, *The Friend*, Chicago: University of Chicago Press, 2007.

Fairweather, Janet (trans.), *Liber Eliensis: A History of the Isle of Ely from the Seventh Century to the Twelfth, compiled by a Monk of Ely in the Twelfth Century*, Martlesham: Boydell and Brewer, 2005.

Harris, Mark, *Grave Matters*, Scribner, 2007.

Larkin, Philip, 'Church Going', 'An Arundel Tomb', *Collected Poems*, London: Faber and Faber, 1988.

Louthan, Howard, 'Tongues, Toes, and Bones: Remembering Saints in Early Modern Bohemia', in *Relics and Remains: Past and Present Supplement* 5, ed. Alexandra Walsham, Oxford: Oxford University Press, 2010, 167–83, 172–3.

Taylor, Jeremy, *The Whole Works of the Right Rev. Jeremy Taylor: The Rule and Exercises of Holy Living and Dying*, ed. Charles Eden, Charleston, SC: BiblioBazaar, 2010.

Tillich, Paul, *The Courage to Be*, London: Collins, 1984.

Traherne, Thomas, *Inducements to Retiredness*, in vol. 1, *The Works of Thomas Traherne*, ed. Jan Ross, Cambridge: D. S. Brewer, 2005.

For more information on green burial innovations:
www.honeycreekwoodlands.com
www.eternalreefs.com
Ramsey Creek Preserve: www.memorialecosystems.com

Woollen coffins:
www.naturallegacy.com

Woodland burial sites in the UK:
St Albans Woodland Burial Trust www.woodlandburialtrust.com

Acknowledgments

Every reasonable effort has been made to trace copyright holders of material reproduced in this book, but if any have been inadvertently overlooked the Publishers would be glad to hear from them.

'The Road Not Taken' from *The Poetry of Robert Frost* by Robert Frost (Edited by Edward Connery Latham). Published by Jonathan Cape. Reprinted by permission of The Random House Group Ltd. Published in the USA by Henry Holt and Company.

'An Arundel Tomb' and 'Church Going' from *Collected Poems* by Philip Larkin (Edited by Anthony Thwaite). Published by Faber & Faber. Published in the USA by Farrar, Straus and Giroux, in *The Complete Poems* by Philip Larkin (Edited by Archie Burnett).

'What lips my lips have kissed, and where, and why (Sonnet XLIII)' from *Poems* by Edna St Vincent Millay. Published by Everyman's Library. The Random House Group Ltd.